Life After Death:

The Laura and Caralyn Yoho Story

Robert "Tim" Yoho

outskirts press

Life After Death: The Laura and Caralyn Yoho Story
All Rights Reserved.
Copyright © 2022 Robert "Tim" Yoho
v3.0

The opinions expressed in this manuscript are solely the opinions of the author and do not represent the opinions or thoughts of the publisher. The author has represented and warranted full ownership and/or legal right to publish all the materials in this book.

This book may not be reproduced, transmitted, or stored in whole or in part by any means, including graphic, electronic, or mechanical without the express written consent of the publisher except in the case of brief quotations embodied in critical articles and reviews.

Outskirts Press, Inc.
http://www.outskirtspress.com

ISBN: 978-1-9772-4820-6

Cover Image: Robert "Tim" Yoho and Shirk Photography

Outskirts Press and the "OP" logo are trademarks belonging to Outskirts Press, Inc.

PRINTED IN THE UNITED STATES OF AMERICA

Life After Death: The Laura and Caralyn Yoho Story
is dedicated to
Caralyn, Nathan, Kara, Aaron, Donna,
and to the memory of Laura Elizabeth Brammeier Yoho.

Table of Contents

Preface	i
Before I Ever Met You	1
Dating the Boss	14
The Engagement	20
The Event—Finding Your Team	25
Remove the Tumor	31
Planning for Family	39
Driving in Clean Air	45
Fighting, Living, Friendship	57
Hail Mary	83

The Baby Shower and Cake	85
End of Life	99
Laying Laura to Rest	107
Life After Death	114
Compassion and Generosity	121
Keeping a Promise: Barbells and the Purple Rose	135
Raising Caralyn	140
Paying It Forward	150
Laura and Nathan	159
Life Goes On	166
Acknowledgements	175

Preface

Family members and friends encouraged me to write about the lives of Laura, Nathan, and Caralyn. I cataloged many documents, photographs, and notes along the way. When I retired from Des Moines University at the end of May 2021, I knew it was time. After taking a few weeks off, I researched the process of writing a book and began to write. I chose not to use a ghost writer or content editor. I wanted the story to be in my own words.

Laura and Nathan were looking forward to their wedding and the rich life they would have together. Both had a passion for health and fitness. Everyone agreed they were a perfect match. Like other young couples, they had dreams and aspirations. They talked about starting their own gym and having a family. Four months before their wedding, Laura suffered what was initially diagnosed as a stroke. After seeking a second opinion, she learned her symptoms were caused by a life-threatening form of brain cancer.

Life After Death chronicles Laura and Nathan's life together throughout Laura's diagnosis, twenty-seven months of treatment, and the birth of their daughter, Caralyn, born through a surrogate four months after Laura's death. It was Laura's best friend since second grade, Kara, already a mother of two children, who volunteered to grant the couple their wish of having a child.

The story is both tragic and inspirational. We witnessed Laura's extraordinary courage, Nathan's unwavering commitment to leave no stone unturned in seeking to save Laura's life while giving her the life she deserved, and the meaning of unconditional friendship.

Segmented into multiple short stories woven together, allows the reader to feel the emotions we experienced throughout Laura's treatment, her death, followed by the birth and raising of Caralyn.

We are grateful for the various forms of support Laura and Nathan received during a very challenging time from many individuals and groups, ranging from financial assistance to the medical care she received at a world class medical institution, confirming the goodness that continues to exist in this world. *Life After Death* provides the opportunity for us to recognize their support and express our appreciation.

At some point in time, everyone will be faced with a life-changing circumstance. I hope sharing Laura and Nathan's story and what we learned from the experience will help others deal with difficult times. I encourage people to seek opportunities to bring comfort to someone, you will be rewarded with a feeling of goodness. True generosity requires nothing in return, other than serving as an example to follow.

On a personal note, in the five years following Laura's diagnosis, in addition to the events in Life After Death, I lost both parents. I continued my usual and customary duties as dean of the College of Podiatric Medicine and Surgery at Des Moines University without interruption, was tasked with duties related to institutional accreditation in 2011 and 2016, programmatic accreditation in the 2014, and served as chair of two boards for professional organizations. It was a challenging five years personally and professionally. I am grateful for the support and patience of my wife, Donna.

Before I Ever Met You

Nathan was born in Warrensville Heights, a suburb of Cleveland, Ohio, on the Winter Solstice in 1982. He was our first and only child. My wife, Donna, worked as a floral designer at a flower shop in Shaker Heights, while I attended the Kent State University College of Podiatric Medicine (KSUCPM), known as the Ohio College of Podiatric Medicine at the time. Following graduation, I completed my residency program in Toledo, Ohio, and then returned to my hometown of Clarion, Pennsylvania, to practice.

Nathan was four at the time we moved to Clarion. He made friends quickly at school and in the neighborhood. At an early age he liked to participate in sports. Baseball and hockey were his favorites. Although he did well in a group setting, there were times when he preferred to be by himself and draw or paint. He had an artistic quality about him from an early age.

After completing a master's degree in biology/microbiology from Duquesne University in Pittsburgh, Pennsylvania, and before attending KSUCPM, I was a research assistant at the University of Pittsburgh's School of Public Health and School of Medicine. I was assigned to a team that worked on the use of interferon in small cell lung cancer. Interferons are proteins that are part of a person's natural defenses. They reduce the growth of a tumor and trigger an antitumor immune response.

I found research interesting but was still uncertain what I wanted to do for a career. After a year, I reached a point where I needed to decide to pursue a PhD or go in another direction. I wanted something that considered my background in playing college sports and my interest in science. I looked at various healthcare professions and felt podiatric medicine would be a good fit. While at KSUCPM, I continued to participate in bench research, improving my research skills.

I enjoyed private practice but knew I would be disappointed in myself professionally if I did not apply the research skills developed in previous positions. After six years of private practice, I felt academic medicine would permit me to continue to practice, teach, and use those skills. We moved to West Des Moines, Iowa, in August 1993. I accepted a faculty position at Des

Moines University. I would later become the dean of the College of Podiatric Medicine and Surgery. Nathan was ten years old at the time of the move.

Nathan had a typical childhood growing up. He did well in adjusting to his new environment. This included moving from a school system with about one hundred students in each class to a school system that graduated close to six hundred students each year. Sports provided him the forum to meet people and develop friendships. He was a good student and was liked by his teachers. In high school, he excelled in multiple sports, particularly baseball, which landed him an athletic scholarship at the University of Iowa.

One thing noticeable about Nathan were the cross section of his friends. He was popular but did not connect himself to any particular group. He valued all people, regardless of their background and means. Nathan made it a point to become friends with individuals who were viewed as outsiders, not part of the jock crowd, those that were mocked or even bullied.

After graduating from Valley West Des Moines High School in 2001, he attended the University of Iowa on a baseball scholarship. Nathan started all four years, earning second-team All-Big Ten his junior year. He played summer baseball between his sophomore and junior year and his junior and senior years in the Northwoods League for the Rochester Honkers, in

Rochester, Minnesota, home to the Mayo Clinic. The Northwoods League is a collegiate wood bat league for division one players.

Nathan was the only player who matriculated at the University of Iowa as a freshman to graduate in four years, taking a heavy load his final semester during the baseball season to help the team with its graduation rate. He graduated with a Bachelor of Arts degree in the spring of 2005 with a major in health and sports. He also minored in the areas of business and art.

Throughout high school and college Nathan dated several girls. His pursuit of a career in baseball did not lend itself to long-term relationships, not knowing where he would be located from year to year.

In June 2005, he went undrafted. Everyone was surprised considering the number of teams that expressed serious interest in him. Not to be denied, Nathan attended several tryouts in the Midwest and was signed by the Milwaukee Brewers. In late June, he reported to the Brewers training facility in Phoenix, Arizona. The Brewers assigned him to the Arizona Rookie League, where he played centerfield. He roomed with Michael Brantley, an eighteen-year-old drafted out of high school. Michael played left field. He came from a baseball family. His father had played professional baseball and later coached for the Seattle Mariners. Lorenzo Cain played right field. The Brewers drafted

Lorenzo out of a junior college in Florida. Both Michael and Lorenzo would later be selected as Major League Baseball All-Stars on multiple occasions.

Nathan had an excellent first season in Arizona and was promoted toward the end of the season to the next level, "A ball," with the West Virginia Power in Charleston, a member of the well-established South Atlantic League. The Power roster included many players who eventually made it to Major League Baseball.

For the 2006 season, the Brewers assigned Nathan to the West Virginia Power along with Michael and Lorenzo. A fourth outfielder, Darren Ford, also drafted in 2005, joined the team as well. Darren played many years in the minor leagues. A highlight of his career would be playing for the San Francisco Giants when they won the 2010 World Series. Nathan struggled with a hand injury and played a part-time role in the outfield during the 2006 season. He would return for the 2007 spring training camp.

Following the 2006 season, Nathan stayed with his uncle, my brother Frank, in Charlotte, North Carolina, working for a large accounting firm. He spent time at a local fitness center to prepare for the 2007 season. During that summer, Nathan became interested in the training and business aspect of fitness.

The Brewers moved him around during spring training but did not have a roster position for him at a higher level. They considered keeping Nathan in the spring training facility to see if a position would become available. In the end, he was released. Nathan's next step was to continue his baseball career in an independent baseball league.

During his time in Major League-affiliated baseball, Nathan learned much about the hardships of some of his teammates. A high percent hailed from Venezuela or the Dominican.

Others came from families of modest means. His experience in cultural awareness was firsthand. He valued the experience and came to be viewed by team management and teammates as a mentor.

After being released by the Brewers, Nathan signed with the Slippery Rock Sliders (Slippery Rock, Pennsylvania) of the Frontier League. This worked out well as he had family he could stay with living ten miles away. During the season he was traded to the Florence Freedom (Florence, Kentucky) where he finished out the year with a solid performance. When his third season of professional baseball ended, he returned to West Des Moines.

Nathan and I talked about his future. I was aware of his interest in fitness and suggested he reach out to

Aspen Fitness, one of the larger local fitness centers in Des Moines. Aspen hired Nathan as a personal trainer in October 2007. He completed all the requisite certifications and quickly built a dedicated client base who enjoyed working with him.

During the off-season, Florence traded Nathan to the Laredo Broncos (Laredo, Texas) of the United Baseball League. Independent league baseball players do not make a lot of money and Texas was a long way from home. Things were going well for Nathan at Aspen. At that point, he decided to end his professional baseball career—no doubt an exceedingly difficult decision for him. Baseball had been a big part of Nathan's life. The experience of playing professionally was well worth delaying any other career. But he had found his new passion in the fitness industry.

Born in Davenport, Iowa, to Lenore and Doug Brammeier, Laura was the second of three children: older brother Joe, a gregarious fellow, and younger sister Katy, who had a quiet, more reserved personality. Laura brought balance to the trio.

Laura grew up in the small rural town of Wilton, located midway between Iowa City and Davenport. Doug, an auto mechanic, owned a successful service station business. Family members helped with the business while locals gathered in the waiting area to discuss the local politics of the day. The Brammeiers were well respected and involved in the Wilton community. To this day, they are known for their hospitality to friends and neighbors.

Laura's childhood could be described as what you would expect being raised in small-town Iowa, represented by Norman Rockwell's illustrations of American culture. She attended Wilton community schools from kindergarten through high school. Laura liked to keep busy by participating in various youth sports programs and other community activities, including her involvement in the Girl Scouts. Lenore served as the local troop leader, the Brammeier home being the gathering place.

She met Kara in first grade. The two became best friends in second grade. The relationship only grew as they progressed through the elementary grades, junior high, and high school. Kara was an excellent athlete in high school, playing a variety of sports—typical for a small-town high school that graduated under one hundred students annually. She was particularly gifted in volleyball. Laura played volleyball her sophomore year, mostly to be with Kara rather than for a love of the game. After that, she began to concentrate on fitness, focusing on a combination of nutrition, running, and lifting weights.

Both were popular in high school. That did not necessarily translate to their individual groups of friends.

Kara chummed with the jock crowd while Laura, more the social group. Kara mentioned how they had different friends but the two of them remained best friends. She felt this is what made the relationship they had so unique and special.

After graduating from high school in 2001, Kara planned to attend the University of Iowa. Laura decided she would enroll at St. Ambrose University (SAU). In the spring of their senior year, Laura suggested to Kara that she join her in an orientation session at SAU. It was clearly a tactic to have Kara change her mind. Kara attended the orientation, learned about the volleyball team, and decided to enroll at SAU with her best friend. Laura's strategy worked. The two would room together nearly the entire time at SAU.

A more formal first-year student orientation scheduled over the summer put Laura into contact with Nichole, who came from a town in Illinois, just across the Mississippi River. She and Laura hit it off from the start. Laura reached out to Kara to see if she would agree to Nichole being the third roommate. Kara agreed. During their time at SAU, Hannah, Lindsay, and Jenni were added to the group. The six of them became the best of friends—friends for life. But nothing would ever rise to the relationship between Laura and Kara.

As so often happens, Laura went in one direction and

her high school boyfriend in another direction. Distance and new environments tend to have that effect on high school relationships. Laura continued to see other guys at SAU but nothing that would be long term.

Laura enjoyed the social aspect of college but continued to develop a passion for nutrition and fitness to the point where she badgered people about their eating and workout habits. Laura cared about people's health. She graduated from SAU in 2001, magna cum laude, with a Bachelor of Arts degree in exercise science and health. She was the first member of her family to graduate from college—a proud moment for her parents.

After graduation, she accepted a position as a personal trainer with Aspen Fitness in Cedar Rapids, Iowa. To start working in the position she quickly completed the required certifications, adding a few advanced credentials.

During her time in Cedar Rapids, Laura quickly proved her skills in helping people improve their overall health and well-being. Management took notice and gave her the opportunity to become a Fitness Manager at another Aspen Fitness in Clive, Iowa. She willingly accepted the promotion, looking forward to the next step in her professional development and what life would bring.

The move also helped Laura put a relationship she was having with an individual behind her. A relationship her friends encouraged her to end.

A photo album and video titled, "Before I Ever Met You," were created in advance of Laura and Nathan's wedding. Both take the viewer through various milestones in each of their lives. Each topic begins with the statement, "*Before I ever met you . . .*" The following are several selections from the album and video:

Nathan: I was baptized into St. Michael's the Arch Angel Catholic Church in Butler, PA.

Laura: I was baptized into St. Mary's Catholic Church in Wilton, IA.

Nathan: My mom said I was the cutest baby ever!

Laura: My mom said I was the cutest baby ever!

Nathan: Birthdays always meant cake.

Laura: My favorite part of my birthday was the cake.

Nathan: I went to the shore on vacations.

Laura: I went to the shore on vacations.

Nathan: I got my first pet; it was a kitten named Kitt.

Laura: I got my first pet; it was a dog named Butch.

Nathan: In the summer of 1990, before I ever met you, we went to Disney World and I got an autograph from Chip.

Laura: In the summer of 1990, before I ever met you, we went to Disney World and I got an autograph from Dale. Maybe that is where we first met!

Nathan: I liked to fish with my dad.

Laura: I liked to fish with my dad.

Nathan: I wore a black turtleneck with a blue sweater in my fifth grade picture. I never wore one again.

Laura: I wore a black turtleneck with a blue sweater in my fifth grade picture. I never wore one again.

Nathan: My favorite sport was baseball.

Laura: I just played baseball because my dad made me a malt after every game.

Nathan: I played every sport I could. Baseball was my favorite.

Laura: I played every sport. If I didn't, I would have to get a job.

Nathan: I thought I only wanted to date blondes.

Laura: I knew I only wanted to date a jock.

Nathan: I was a Homecoming King candidate. I didn't win.

Laura: I was a Homecoming Queen candidate. I didn't win.

Nathan: I went to the University of Iowa. I majored in Health and Sport Studies, was captain of the baseball team, and studied some of the time.

Laura: I went to St. Ambrose University. I majored in Strength and Human Performance, was the conditioning coach for the baseball team, and studied all the time.

The album and video go on about meeting each other's family, ending with the engagement.

Dating the Boss

In December 2007, Laura became the Fitness Manager at Aspen Fitness on Hickman Road in Clive, a suburb of Des Moines. She bought a townhouse in Grimes, close to her place of work. Family helped with the move from Cedar Rapids. She also continued personal training at Aspen.

Nathan, several months into working at Aspen after completing the 2007 baseball season, had a new boss. He reported to Laura. He was living with Donna and myself in West Des Moines. In June, he would move into an apartment nearby with his cousin, Jared, a podiatric medical student at Des Moines University. Donna and I were empty nesters again—at least that is what we thought.

Aside from team meetings, if a personal trainer received good evaluations and produced, there was no need to meet with the supervisor on an individual basis. Laura had recently ended a relationship. Nathan happened to be in the market. A mutual client suggested, half-jokingly, to each of them in separate conversations, they should start dating each other.

Nathan laughed it off—after all, he was a direct report to Laura as his supervisor. Laura, on the other hand, approached Nathan and shared the recommendation the mutual client had suggested to her. Possibly to see his reaction? He informed her he had received the same comment.

There was no opposition to the idea, which advanced their relationship to the flirtation phase, each willing to play along.

Kara recalls Laura being excited about the possibility of dating Nathan. Laura provided a physical description of him as, "a looker," and offered up some personal information. The background check included something to the effect that he had played baseball. Kara admitted she looked Nathan up on the internet. She commented on his good looks and corrected Laura, "He was a terrific baseball player." Laura did not pay much attention to his athletic credentials.

The first time Kara met Nathan occurred when the

SAU girls came to Des Moines to enjoy the sights and sounds of the city. Laura asked Nathan if he would drive them around. He agreed. Kara described him as quiet, funny, and good-looking. From what she heard from Laura and from this initial encounter, Kara, much like most people, had a good feeling about the two of them.

Their first official date happened when Laura's supervisor, a co-owner of Aspen Fitness, asked Laura and Nathan to join him at a mixed martial arts event in Des Moines on July 26, 2008. They enjoyed each other's company more so than the rough and tumble action in the ring. It opened the door to a relationship beyond supervisor/employee.

As with most relationships, theirs just evolved over time. They liked the night life Des Moines had to offer, attending concerts, eating out, and meeting each other's friends. They particularly enjoyed working out together during off hours, which eventually led both to join the gym CrossFit 515. One of the more favorite activities would be for the two of them to just hang out at Laura's or Nathan's place. When their relationship became public, management transferred Laura to a new location in the greater Des Moines area. She would no longer supervise Nathan.

Donna and I first met Laura in the late fall of 2008. Nathan invited Laura to our home for a casual evening together. Nathan was not in the habit of bringing the girls he dated to our home.

We immediately sensed something different. Donna and I are reserved by nature. We connected with her from the very start. It seemed so natural for Donna and Laura to carry on a conversation about any number of subjects. We received a thank-you card from Laura after that first encounter. We received another card in January 2009 thanking us for the bracelet Donna had picked out as a Christmas gift and for us being so welcoming to her. Most of our time with the couple over the next year and a half involved them visiting us or the four of us going out to dinner.

Seeing how well they meshed, and given our positive feelings about Laura, we invited her to travel to the Outer Banks in North Carolina for a July 2010 summer vacation with members of Donna's family. The vacation gave Laura the opportunity to meet Nathan's relatives. She fit right in. They swam together in the Atlantic Ocean, ran up and down the sand dunes of Kitty Hawk, and viewed the wild horses of Corolla.

Laura introduced Nathan to her family by visiting Lenore, Doug, and her siblings at her home in Wilton. Reserved would not apply in the case of the Brammeiers, especially with Laura's brother Joe. Nathan could hold his own, but it could be a challenge to keep up with the various activities that may be going on simultaneously in the Brammeier household. A tap was in the kitchen area and a shot of Grey Goose was available upon request. Any game played involved an exchange of money. Nathan enjoyed Laura's family, although they noted he was quiet. It was more likely him being overwhelmed, combined with his restrained personality. He quickly appreciated the closeness of Laura to her parents and siblings. A frequent family activity for the Brammeiers was heading to Davenport and the casinos. Nathan was adept at Blackjack and had a few successful payouts, which no doubt were announced to the casino patrons by Joe.

Donna and I first met Lenore and Doug at the Funny Bone Comedy Club in West Des Moines. Laura and Nathan arranged a dinner/entraintment outing for the six of us. Further introductions followed as we moved to the Blue Moon Dueling Piano Bar—not exactly what Donna and I envisioned to meet our son's girlfriend's parents for the first time. Needless to say, the environment for an initial encounter was a little on the awkward side. Doug admitted he had looked Nathan up on the internet and confirmed that I, in fact, served as a dean at Des Moines University.

We could check meeting the parents off the list. Everyone could tell Laura and Nathan's relationship was special.

Both Laura and Nathan continued to make a name for themselves in the fitness business.

Nathan received the 2009 Aspen Fitness Trainer of the Year Award and Laura was featured in the lead article of the 2009 Health Issue of Seasons Magazine, a publication of the Hy-Vee Corporation, covering food, lifestyle, and health with circulation throughout the Midwest. At the same time their relationship continued to grow.

In the summer of 2009, Nathan purchased a quaint three-level, three-bedroom home not far from Laura's townhome. Laura moved in with Nathan in January 2010 and used her place as a rental. The Brammeiers and Yohos were anxious for the next step.

The Engagement

Every groom-to-be wants their proposal to be a memorable experience for their bride-to-be. Nathan was no different. After two years of dating, Nathan had no doubt that Laura was the one. Once he decided to take the plunge, the next step was to notify Laura's parents. It wasn't a matter of asking permission in the traditional sense; his approach was that of informing Lenore and Doug of his intention. The Brammeiers had gotten to know Nathan and recognized how happy Laura was when they were together. Lenore and Doug were excited for the couple and this next big step in their relationship.

Next on the list was the engagement ring. Nathan's friend, Scot, who would serve as his best man, recommended he reach out to Mike at Josephs Jewelers in

Des Moines. Josephs, a locally owned family business for five generations, had a reputation for its exceptional service and quality. Nathan followed through on Scot's suggestion and worked with Mike to find the perfect ring for Laura. Nathan did not consult with anyone else about the type or style of ring. He felt he knew Laura's taste well enough to make the decision.

After purchasing the ring, Nathan commissioned a friend and local artist, Jon, to paint a portrait of the ring. The painting measured approximately 16" by 16". It was an excellent portrayal of the ring.

There are trails that run through Grimes. An access point to a trail Laura and Nathan frequently ran was close to Nathan's home. The trail is flat at the access point. Moving in a southern direction, the trail makes a sharp turn to the right, which starts an incline to the west until reaching the grounds of the Grimes United Methodist Church. A large oak tree is situated to the right of the bend as the trail approaches the incline. It is highly visible to individuals on the trail and would offer the perfect location to implement Nathan's plan.

Nathan enlisted the help of Scot to hang the painting on the oak tree with the ring secured to the back of the painting. They did their best to synchronize their duties. An unwitting resident in the neighborhood was on her deck and saw a man armed with a hammer running through the wooded area. Scot ducked behind a tree as a young couple was approaching the turn. The woman grabbed her camera. Her initial thought was the man was up to some type of nefarious activity as his victims approached his hiding area. Just before shouting a warning to the couple, she realized what was going on and started to snap off photographs. She captured the surprised look on Laura's face, Nathan's smile, and the hug followed by a kiss. Laura accepted his proposal.

The neighbor let Laura and Nathan know she caught all the action on film and would send them the photographs. To this day, the nails securing the painting of the ring remain in the tree, a reminder of that terrific moment in time.

Laura owned a cat, Oliver. She had informed Nathan it would be nice if Oliver had a companion, orange being the preferred color. Nathan let her know one cat was enough. But it just so happened that one of Nathan's clients mentioned she had recently found a kitten on her doorstep and was unable to find the owner, or the owner did not want to be found. The kitten met the color requirement. Timing is everything.

Nathan offered to adopt the kitten. He asked Donna and me to keep the kitten at our house until the day of the engagement. We delivered the orange bundle of fur while Nathan and Laura were out on the run. He was waiting for them on their return. He came to be known as Lou, named after Laura's paternal grandfather. Nathan had fulfilled Laura's request: an orange playmate for Oliver.

The final event of engagement day was taking Laura out for a celebration dinner at a local restaurant. At least that is what Laura thought. Nathan had reached out to Laura's parents, her brother, sister, and to Donna and myself. We were invited to the celebration dinner. Laura rarely cried, and when she saw everyone gathered to celebrate her and Nathan's engagement, she had tears of pure happiness. It was a fun evening and a chance for all of us to get to know each other a little better. Much of the talk was about the wedding and the wonderful life they would have together. It was one of the best days of their lives.

Joe Brammeier, ever looking for material for Laura and Nathan's wedding, heard about the details of the engagement and suggested a reenactment of the engagement process be captured on video that could be played at the wedding reception. Nathan and Laura were agreeable. Joe contacted a friend who was a videographer to produce the video. The video shows Nathan working with Mike to select the ring, Jon painting the portrait of the ring, intermingled with short clips of Laura at work as a personal trainer, Scot hiding behind a tree, and ending with Laura hugging Nathan after receiving the ring.

The video was included in Joe's wedding reception extravaganza. But that was not the end of the video. The chief executive officer of Josephs Jewelers viewed the reenactment and asked permission to use the video as the inaugural presentation in their Gold Box Moment Campaign created to highlight special engagement scenarios. Permission granted.

The Event—Finding Your Team

Laura and Nathan enjoyed the holidays with family. They made it through a typical cold Iowa winter. March 15, 2011 was an unusually warm day with temperatures near 70 degrees. Just five months until the wedding and plans were underway.

Around 4:00 p.m. I received a phone call from Donna. She had just gotten off the phone with Laura. Donna was concerned about Laura. She described how Laura seemed anxious and struggled to form sentences. Laura said something about passing out and being confused. Donna instructed Laura to call 911 for assistance and let her know she would contact Nathan. Donna headed to Grimes. I left work and drove directly to Nathan's home.

When I arrived, EMTs were administering to Laura. Donna arrived a few minutes before I did. Laura's vital signs were stable and she was alert to time and place. The EMTs were comfortable with us taking Laura to a new hospital in West Des Moines that was part of a large healthcare system. It took ten minutes to make the drive. Laura struggled to form complete sentences as we transported her to the hospital.

We arrived at the emergency department where we met Nathan. Laura was processed quickly and evaluated by the emergency room physician. Laura described feeling faint while exercising, felt confused, and experienced difficulty forming words. A magnetic resonance image (MRI) of her head identified an "abnormal area" measuring 2.6 cm in the transverse plane (side-to-side), 1.6 cm in the anterior-posterior plane (front-to-back), and 1.2 cm in the craniocaudal plane (up-and-down) located in the left supramarginal gyrus, consistent an acute nonhemorrhagic event.

The supramarginal gyrus, located in the upper outside of both sides of the brain, is part of the somatosensory cortex which interprets tactile sensory data and is involved in the perception of space and limb location. It may also play a role in language perception and processing. Lesions in this area may cause receptive aphasia (inability to speak) and difficulty understanding written and spoken language. Acute nonhemorrhagic refers to a recent, nonbleeding event.

The physician informed us Laura had a stroke. She would need to be admitted to the hospital for further evaluation, monitoring, and management. Laura was transported by ambulance to the primary medical center of the healthcare system and admitted under the medicine service.

The next morning, Laura was seen by internal medicine and neurology. A magnetic resonance angiogram (MRA), a study to assess blood flow, failed to identify any abnormality of the cervical (neck) or intracranial blood vessels. A transesophageal electrocardiogram and additional cardiac tests were also noncontributory. Her blood work did suggest the possibility of a hypercoagulable condition called prothrombin G20210A mutation.

The prothrombin condition is a genetic disorder that increases the risk of forming blood clots, especially in the deep veins of the legs. This can result in a pulmonary embolism, where the clot breaks free and travels to the lungs. It can be potentially fatal. Having this prothrombin abnormality increases the risk of a blood clot from 1 in 1,000 in individuals without the condition, to 2.5 in 1,000 per year in individuals who have the condition. Fortunately, most people with the prothrombin disorder never develop a blood clot in their lifetime.

Laura was discharged after a two-day hospitalization, placed on a daily aspirin, and referred to a hematology/oncology medical group.

Over the next five weeks, Laura was seen on two occasions by a hematologist/oncologist. He continued to focus on the prothrombin mutation while she continued to experience several episodes of lightheadedness and difficulty speaking. In the words of Laura, "He would not listen to what I was saying." In frustration and with the support of Nathan and family, Laura sought a second opinion.

Enter Dr. Angela Sandre, another physician in the same hematology/oncology group. Seen on April 25, a follow-up MRI was ordered and reconfirmed the presence of a mass in the supramarginal gyrus of the left temporal lobe more suggestive of a primary brain neoplasm, not the previously suspected stroke. From the first appointment, Laura expressed her comfort and confidence in Dr. Sandre. She had found her local physician.

Dr. Sandre immediately referred Laura to a local neurosurgeon who, based on Laura's history, physical examination, and review of the MRIs, recommended she see Dr. Ian Parney, a highly respected neurosurgeon at the Mayo Clinic in Rochester, Minnesota. Dr. Parney specialized in the treatment of gliomas, glioblastomas, other primary malignant brain tumors, metastatic brain tumors, and meningiomas. Dr. Parney was an experienced surgeon in dealing with brain cancers.

Laura and Nathan met Dr. Parney on May 9. He had thoroughly reviewed Laura's medical record and the numerous studies in advance of the appointment. Dr. Parney took his time with Laura to review her history and perform his own assessment. In his opinion, Laura's condition was a malignant tumor, brain cancer. After allowing the news to sink in, Laura wanted to know the next step. Dr. Parney offered three treatment options: observation with serial MRIs, left frameless stereotactic biopsy, or left frontotemporal craniotomy with resection of the tumor using frameless stereotactic guidance. The risks and benefits were discussed for each option. Laura and Nathan made the decision to go with the most definitive of the three, craniotomy with surgical resection of the tumor. The surgery would take place in four days.

Dr. Parney was everything they expected; he was friendly, experienced, and presented information in a manner they could understand. Laura had found her surgeon.

The next day, Laura and Nathan met Dr. Joon Uhm, a neuro-oncologist at the Mayo Clinic. Dr. Uhm's areas of expertise and interests included patients afflicted with tumors of the brain and spine, clinical trials to evaluate promising new drugs and approaches in neuro-oncology, and optimizing quality of life for patients by integrating his experiences as a neurologist and oncologist.

Laura and Nathan felt the initial appointment with Dr. Uhm seemed a little rushed. Dr. Uhm was in complete agreement with Dr. Parney and supportive of the decision to surgically resect the mass. Dr. Uhm planned to be out of town but would schedule a follow-up appointment with Laura after her surgery. Further treatment would be based on the pathology report. He wished them the best. Laura and Nathan were not completely sure of Dr. Uhm, but if Dr. Parney recommended him, that was good enough. Little did Laura, Nathan, and Dr. Uhm know the relationship they would develop.

The main medical providers in Laura's treatment were now in place. Laura and Nathan would stay in Rochester until she was discharged after her surgery. The journey to survive was about to begin.

Remove the Tumor

The Brammeiers and Yohos descended on Rochester the day before Laura's surgery. Laura and Nathan appeared to be holding up well. They had a positive outlook and were looking forward to having the procedure completed and returning home as soon as possible. Everyone stayed at a Marriott Hotel in close proximity to St. Mary's Hospital, the facility where Laura would undergo the craniotomy and tumor resection. Nathan stayed with Laura at the hospital.

Laura's brother Joe, who was in the fitness equipment business by day and a practicing standup comedian during the remainder of the time, kept everyone distracted from the seriousness of the moment.

Donna and I were familiar with Rochester. There were

trails throughout the city along the South Fork Zumbro River that provided a respite from waiting or just the opportunity for prayer and reflection. The baseball stadium, Mayo Field, built in 1951, is located along one of the trails.

Mayo Field is a mainstay of sports in the downtown area with its old rusty cast iron seating behind home plate. Nathan played baseball at Mayo Field the summers of 2003 and 2004. We would recall Nathan, wearing the aqua and white uniforms with the goose logo, making a diving catch in the outfield or lining a ball over the short right field fence. Those were fun days. We never anticipated returning to Rochester on a different mission.

During his second season with the Honkers, Nathan lived with a couple, Gary and Donna. They had two young sons. The boys loved to be with Nathan and his teammates, who frequently came over to the house. That family would become friends for life, attending Nathan's major life events occurring over the next several years.

It was around 6:00 a.m. on May 13. Everyone gathered at St. Mary's Hospital to see Laura before she was transported to the operating room. Dr. Parney reminded us there was always some degree of uncertainty with brain surgery, including temporary or even permanent loss of certain abilities of the patient. We appreciated his honesty. Nathan was the last to leave Laura's side. They parted with a double kiss. He maintained a positive outlook, but you could feel the sadness in his heart over what had transpired to the love of his life over the past two months.

The official description of the procedure was a left frontotemporal craniotomy with resection of lesion using frameless stereotactic guidance, also referred to as neuro-navigation. This is the process by which neurosurgeons use MRI or computerized tomography (CT) imaging studies, targeted algorithms, and a computer workstation to precisely locate and target a tumor or other lesion inside the brain. In the past it required a frame secured to the patient's head, hence the term frameless.

The procedure would take between four to six hours to complete. During that time family members relied on Joe to keep everyone occupied. As usual, Joe was successful in keeping the mood upbeat. He organized a competitive tournament of every game in the neurosurgery waiting room. Joe eventually proclaimed himself champion and made sure everyone, including strangers, were aware of his title.

A member of the St. Mary's staff periodically provided a progress report, always positive. At around the four-hour mark, we were informed the surgery was over and Laura had been transferred to the post-anesthesia care unit. Family members were escorted to a counseling room where Dr. Parney would meet with everyone.

Dr. Parney is what you would imagine from a neurosurgeon. He deals with some of the most serious conditions that are life-changing and life-threatening. His demeanor was very businesslike, but that is what you expect and want from a neurosurgeon. He let us know Laura was awake and doing well. The procedure went as planned and he felt confident the lesion was removed. He did temper his comments by informing us it appeared to be a cancerous mass. A definitive diagnosis would be provided by the pathologist after microscopic analysis of the removed tissue.

Once awake and alert, Laura moved to the neurosurgical intensive care unit for observation and pain management. It was truly remarkable seeing Laura later that day. She was in good spirits, had minimal pain, and experienced no complications with her speech. There appeared to be no observable affects related to the tumor or procedure. The look on everyone's face was that of relief. The following day she was transferred to the neurosurgical floor. Nathan stayed with Laura throughout her hospitalization.

As they say in medicine, Laura's hospital course was uneventful. Major brain surgery on May 13 and discharged on May 16. She would see Dr. Uhm for the second time on May 24. The next step would be determined by the pathology report.

Laura returned to Grimes with a comprehensive list of postoperative instructions. To ensure compliance, when Nathan worked, Donna would stand watch over her. Laura's strength, motivation, and courage were incredible. She had to be frequently reminded to ease off exercising. Laura was doing so well; rather than asking about the pathology report, waiting to find out in person seemed to the best approach. Out of sight, out of mind.

Laura, Nathan, Lenore, and Donna left in the early morning for the three-hour trip to Rochester. Dr. Uhm shared the final pathology report, a grade III anaplastic astrocytoma. There is some confusion in the medical literature as to the difference between an astrocytoma and a glioma.

Both arise from the same cell type, with the glioma considered an advanced grade IV lesion. The terms are sometimes used interchangeably. Regardless, Laura's diagnosis was serious and life-threatening. As hard as it was to hear the diagnosis, Dr. Parney had prepared everyone to anticipate such an outcome. Dr. Uhm noted the postoperative MRI showed complete resection of the lesion. Other positive indicators were Laura's overall excellent health, normal neurologic exam, and her Eastern Cooperative Oncology Group (ECOG) performance score was 0. The ECOG score meant Laura was fully active and she had no restriction on activities in the sense that someone can do everything they were able to do prior to their diagnosis. The ECOG provides as quantifiable monitoring tool for measuring a patient's functional status.

Brain cancer treatment, like many cancer treatments, follows prescribed protocols based on clinical research outcomes. Radiation therapy is the mainstay of therapy for grade III brain tumors following resection. For grade IV tumors, daily low dose Temozolomide is added to the treatment protocol. Temozolomide is in a class of medications called alkylating agents. It works by slowing or stopping the growth of cancer cells in the body. Even through there was no straightforward evidence that adding Temozolomide to the treatment regimen was superior to radiation alone, Dr. Uhm recommended it be added to Laura's treatment. Laura and Nathan unanimously approved the recommendation.

To make informed decisions, Nathan decided early on he would learn as much as possible about brain cancer, brain cancer treatments, and the potential side effects of those treatments. Nathan became aware of the concern with use of Temozolomide and how this might affect Laura's ability to carry a child. With this in mind, an option could be for Laura to participate in ovarian stimulation with subsequent creation of embryos. The process consists of administering hormones designed to stimulate several ovarian follicles at the same time to yield an increased number of oocytes to fertilize into embryos. This would require acting sooner than later to stay on track for Laura's radiation therapy and the Temozolomide. A maximum five-week window existed until the next phase of Laura's treatment needed to start.

The appointment ended with Laura and Nathan planning to discuss the ovarian stimulation option with family and arrive at a decision. That decision would determine when the six-week combination of radiation therapy and chemotherapy would begin. To reduce travel, Dr. Uhm's office worked with Dr. Sandre's office to coordinate Laura's treatments. Laura and Nathan had already made up their minds about ovarian stimulation.

On the return trip to Grimes, Laura and Nathan called other family members and provided an update with further details to follow. I sensed both Laura and Nathan felt much better about Dr. Uhm. Although he noted the seriousness of her diagnosis, Dr. Uhm emphasized the favorable prognostic indicators and thoroughly reviewed the treatment plan moving forward.

Over that first weekend following the surgery, I spoke to Nathan in private about Laura's diagnosis. I had taken the time to research as much as I could about anaplastic astrocytomas.

Nathan had done the same. As his father, I felt obligated to ask him if he considered delaying the wedding to see how Laura responded to the treatments. Father to son, man to man, he responded by saying, "Every woman deserves a wedding, especially Laura." I felt terrible about asking the question. The topic never came up again.

Planning for Family

Medical ovarian stimulation is a complex process dependent on timing and the administration of certain hormones, namely follicle stimulating hormone (FSH) and luteinizing hormone (LH).

This step in the in vitro fertilization (IVF) process is where the egg-producing ability of a female is intentionally supercharged, leading to the production of a higher number of eggs compared to a typical ovulation cycle. FSH injections maintain higher levels of hormone in the body, stimulating ovarian follicles to develop during the menstrual cycle, thus allowing the ovaries to produce more mature eggs. Just before ovulation, higher levels of estrogen induce a spike in LH, which results in ovulation. A "trigger shot" of a large dose of human chorionic gonadotropin (HCG) is administered to stimulate the onset of ovulation.

The stimulation phase involves the administration of hormones for eight to fourteen days, inducing the ovaries to produce many eggs. This is followed by a procedure to retrieve the eggs in preparation for fertilization and reimplantation or cryopreservation.

Laura and Nathan quickly decided to proceed with ovarian stimulation and IVF in hopes that one day Laura would be able to carry. They sought consultation from a highly respected fertility practice in Des Moines. The practice was sensitive to Laura's medical condition and the urgency to complete the process in a short window so that she might start her cancer treatments in a timely manner.

With the initial appointment, the fertility physician reviewed Laura's medical history, completed a physical exam, and performed a baseline ultrasound. Several blood samples were drawn to assess Laura's fertility status. Nathan also completed a required screening process as the male donor. They received counseling on what to expect and agreed to proceed to the next step.

Within a week, Laura was approved to proceed with ovarian stimulation. Nathan would administer the hormone injections while the fertility team closely monitored Laura's response.

Laura went about her daily activities with the only

restriction being to limit her exercising, which she was already advised to do following her surgery.

After ten days of receiving hormonal therapy, Laura received the HCG trigger injection. The egg-retrieval process needed to take place within thirty-six hours of the HCG injection. This occurred the following day.

The retrieval process went as planned. It was performed as an office-based outpatient procedure and lasted approximately thirty minutes. Under light sedation and using ultrasound-directed aspiration, the physician guided a needle into Laura's ovaries to locate the mature follicles. Once accessed, the needle punctured each follicle. The eggs and fluid inside each follicle were aspirated in the needle. Once harvested, an embryologist would evaluate the fluid and identify the most viable eggs for fertilization.

Toward the end of the stimulation process, Laura began to experience a feeling of abdominal bloating. Two days after the retrieval procedure, the bloating sensation intensified. Laura also began to quickly gain weight and had difficulty urinating. Her symptoms were consistent with Ovarian Hyperstimulation Syndrome (OHSS). OHSS is an exaggerated response to excess hormones occurring in roughly ten percent of individuals undergoing ovarian stimulation. OHSS causes the ovaries to swell, become painful, and leak fluid into the abdominal cavity. The condition is classified as mild, moderate, and severe based on the patient's symptoms, clinical exam, bloodwork, and ultrasound.

Normal ovarian length averages approximately three centimeters and is described as about the size of a walnut. In Laura's case, based on the clinical exam and ultrasound findings, her OHSS was classified as moderate to severe, where her ovaries reached the size of an orange. As the ovary is stimulated and increases in size, fluid leaks from the blood vessels supplying the ovaries into the abdomen. The buildup of fluid in the abdomen is referred to as asities. This is manifested by abdominal bloating, pain, sudden weight gain, and kidney problems. Laura had preexisting risk factors for OHSS being under thirty years of age and of slight stature, combined with the urgency to complete the process as quickly as possible.

On three occasions, within a brief period of time, a paracentesis procedure needed to be performed to alleviate Laura's symptoms. With this procedure, a syringe is inserted into the abdomen to remove excessive fluid. It is common to drain between one to two litters of fluid each time. This was the case for Laura. She described the discomfort from the paracentesis to be much less than the pain from the pressure. Relief was immediate.

The final time the procedure was performed, Donna and I were helping with yard work at Nathan's home, something we were doing regularly on weekends. Nathan was at work. Laura began to experience mild bloating and pressure pain. Within several hours her symptoms advanced from mild to severe in intensity. Laura's abdomen became enlarged to the point where outside observers would think she was in the third trimester of pregnancy. Donna called the fertility office and was transferred to the on-call physician who happened to be on the golf course.

On the ride to the office, Laura was in the front seat and Donna in the back seat. I touched Laura's abdomen and was shocked at the degree of firmness. You could appreciate her pain. We promptly arrived at the office. After a fifteen-minute wait, we were greeted by the physician. I can only imagine what he was thinking. We looked like we had just finished plowing the lower forty. At first, he seemed somewhat irritated over the interruption. After seeing Laura's condition, he knew his golf game could wait.

Laura never hesitated or expressed regret throughout the ovarian stimulation process, even when enduring the pain from the complication. Having family was important to her. If that was the price, so be it.

The next step was to create the embryos. Embryo formation involves inseminating the egg with the donor's sperm. This is completed shortly after egg retrieval. At five to seven days an embryo develops to where it can be preserved by cryopreservation. This process requires removing water from the cells, replacing it with a cryoprotectant agent to prevent the cells from forming ice crystals, and then freezing them at –320 degrees Fahrenheit. Laura and Nathan had their embryos in hopes that one day Laura would be able to carry a child.

It took five weeks to complete the process. The time had come to start Laura's cancer treatments.

Driving in Clean Air

Treatment following resection of a grade III astrocytoma involves a combination of external beam radiation therapy and chemotherapy. Several steps are required in preparation for radiation therapy. Laura underwent a CT scan to assist in identifying the specific area of her brain to be targeted for the radiation. A head and neck mask for Laura was constructed and fitted to assist the radiation technologist focus on the target area and limit the effect of scatter radiation. The radiation dose administered is based on the location of the lesion and tissue type. These steps are taken to maximize radiation to the target area while minimizing damage to surrounding healthy tissues.

Laura's external beam radiation therapy consisted of five daily administrations per week for six consecutive weeks. Each session, depending on the logistics, lasted between twenty to thirty minutes. This was combined with Laura taking a daily low dose of Temozolomide by mouth over the same six-week period. The radiation therapy was delivered at a local cancer center in Des Moines with Dr. Sandre serving as her local oncologist. Dr. Sandre's office assisted in coordinating Laura's treatments. Aside from the inconvenience of traveling to the cancer center on a daily basis and experiencing a feeling of mild fatigue, Laura tolerated the treatments without complication.

Prior to completing her radiation treatments and chemotherapy, Laura returned to the Mayo Clinic on July 20 for follow-up visits with Drs. Uhm and Parney. Laura had an MRI performed two days prior to the Mayo visit. The MRI demonstrated filling of the cavity created by removal of the tumor without evidence of reoccurrence. Both physicians commented on Laura's exceptional progress clinically, supported by the findings of the MRI. It was an excellent report. At that point, Dr. Parney signed off on Laura's case, barring any new neurosurgical concerns. Laura and Nathan expressed their gratitude to Dr. Parney.

Moving forward, Laura would see Dr. Uhm several weeks after Laura and Nathan's wedding planned for August 13. At that time, Dr. Uhm would start Laura on a six-cycle maintenance dose of Temozolomide.

Each cycle consisted of five consecutive daily doses of Temozolomide by month. Dr. Uhm made it a point to extend his best wishes to the couple on their upcoming big day. He began to take a greater interest in their personal lives.

Tucked neatly between the July and September Mayo appointments were wedding showers and the wedding. One prewedding event stood out in particular: a couple's shower at Nathan's home held two weeks before the wedding. Most memorable activities with the Brammeier family have one thing in common: Joe Brammeier. A carnival atmosphere, beer tents, high-calorie food, corn-hole tournaments, and the purchase of T-shirts with "We Love (heart) Laura" inscribed on the front and "Buck Train Fumors" on the back, proceeds going to Laura and Nathan. They sold out quickly. All coordinated by Joe. It was the first time many of Laura and Nathan's friends had the opportunity to see the couple since she was diagnosed with brain cancer. Laura and Nathan were at the top of their game and feeling good about the upcoming wedding and their future together.

The wedding activities scheduled for August 11–13 were a celebration of Laura's courage and Nathan's devotion—the union of two people so perfect for each other—mixed in with a recognition of family and friends. Thursday, August 11, was the designated travel day. A chance for family members and the wedding party to check into the Radisson Hotel in Davenport, settle in, and prepare for the weekend activities.

Donna and I hosted the rehearsal dinner at an Italian restaurant in Bettendorf on Friday, August 12. Attendees included Laura and Nathan, members of the wedding party, family members, and Father Bob. Spirits were high and you could feel the excitement in the room. I welcomed everyone and expressed my appreciation to those who traveled a long distance to come to Iowa, and to Father Bob, the priest who would be performing the ceremony. In a short period of time, we had grown fond of Father Bob. He was close to retiring from the priesthood and his appointment to St. Mary's Church in Wilton would be his final. He knew of Laura and Nathan's story. Father Bob conveyed what an honor it would be for him to preside over their wedding.

I dedicated much of my talk to the challenges Laura and Nathan faced to get to this weekend. I voiced my admiration for Laura's physical and emotional strength and Nathan's unwavering commitment to Laura's health and well-being. They were meant for each other. It also provided a moment for me to acknowledge the role had Donna played over the past several months. She was the unsung hero, making sure Laura stayed on schedule with her appointments and helping her with the daily duties at home. Donna became the person

Laura could approach and privately share her thoughts and concerns.

Donna and I spent many hours in Grimes, helping in whatever way we could. I shared how I had improved my laundry skills but continued to feel awkward when it came to Laura's lingerie—that is where I drew the line with my soon to be daughter-in-law.

A highlight of the evening happened when Laura and Nathan introduced each member of the wedding party: Katy, Nichole, Kara, Lynn, Brandon, Jared, Matt, Luke, Scott, Andy, and Paul. They shared personal stories about each member of the party. Each received a gift selected specifically for them. Paul, a two-time All-American wrestler at the University of Iowa, and UFC fighter, was a big boxing fan. Nathan gave Paul a set of autographed boxing gloves from the current WBO Welterweight Champion, Manny Pacquiao. Everyone enjoyed seeing the reaction from members of the wedding party to their individualized gift. The evening set the tone for Saturday's main event.

It had been nine months since the engagement. The wedding day finally arrived. It was a sunny day with temperatures in the mid eighties and towering cumulus clouds forming images open to interpretation. Around 10:00 a.m. the photographer and videographer began to capture the activities of the day as they were to unfold. Laura was stunning in her wedding dress and Nathan equally handsome in his tuxedo. The maid of honor and bridesmaids wore blue dresses. The design varied based on individual preference. Nathan, the best man, groomsmen, and ushers wore matching dark blue tuxedos neatly fitted to each man's physique. It could easily have been a photo shoot for Vogue or GQ Magazine.

The emotion, significance, and beauty of the day was captured in a portrait by Ben Shirk of Shirk Photography. The photo was taken in an alley against the background of clouds and powder blue sky. With each looking at the other, Nathan held Laura as she leaned back holding her bouquet of white roses and Calla lilies.

There were very few RSVPs returned where invited guests declined the invitation. Family and guests came from as far away as California, Pennsylvania, Ohio, Arizona, Tennessee, North Carolina, and South Carolina. St. Mary's Church was filled to capacity.

The ceremony lasted approximately forty minutes. Father Bob kept the ceremony on track and spoke about the challenges Laura and Nathan had faced and the importance of prayer as part of her treatment and continued good health. Family members read scripture and Doug's close friend Henry Bentley, owner of Bentley's Funeral Home, came out of retirement to sing, accompanied by his veteran acoustic guitar.

When it came time for the Declaration of Consent, Laura did not wait for her cue from Father Bob to repeat the declaration; she just started right in. Her eagerness was met with approving laughter. Their vows ended with the statement, "I will love you and honor you all the days of my life." Truer words were never spoken.

Laura and Nathan took the time to greet everyone who attended as guests were released row by row. It took a little longer than expected, but then again, it was a chance for Laura and Nathan to express their appreciation for the support they had received over the past four months and for people to see how well Laura was doing. There were many hugs, kisses, and handshakes. The newlyweds exited the church to a shower of tiny bubbles. The service was simple and elegant—everything we had hoped for and more.

We weren't sure what to expect at the reception with Joe Brammeier serving as the host, producer, and director of this part of the wedding. He kept everything close to the vest but made it clear: this was to be the reception to end all receptions. In Joe's word, "Epic."

The evening started with Lenore on her cell phone frantically talking to Joe and Tom, his co-host, relaxing in Joe's father-in-law's man cave a few miles from the venue. Their interaction was broadcast on an oversized video screen set up in the banquet hall.

Lenore asked Joe why he and Tom were not at the reception. Through a miscommunication, Joe thought the reception started an hour later. The video follows Joe and Tom rushing out the door and driving to the front entrance of the Radisson Hotel. Joe took advantage of the valet who offered to park his car—which he gladly agreed too, identifying himself as a guest of the hotel under the name Dr. Tim Yoho. They continued through the lobby and burst through the double doors for an on-time arrival and start to the show.

While waiting on the wedding party, Joe served as the master of ceremony for the "pregame show" highlighted by Laura and Nate's engagement and "Before We Met" videos, a testimonial and gift painting from Jon (the artist who painted the diamond ring involved in the engagement), a cameo appearance and guitar solo from Slash, and a cringe-worthy testimonial from Nathan's paternal grandmother, Nina. These and other pregame festivities filled the time.

Transitioning to the reception, the parents of the couple were introduced, followed by members of the wedding party in a style similar to UFC announcer Bruce Buffer. In preparation for the bride and groom's arrival, Joe Satriani's song "Crowd Chant" was blasted into the room with Laura and Nate's names inserted into key bars of the song. As this was going on, a video was playing of Laura and Nathan running on a dirt road with corn fields on both sides. As they reached the end of the trail, Joe Brammeier had achieved his goal of hyping the audience into a frenzy. They broke through the paper screen and into the banquet hall to a standing ovation. It was an amazing and fitting entrance.

Doug Brammeier welcomed everyone to the reception. He used a nice balance of emotion and humor as he reflected on his daughter and new son-in-law. The usual and customary toasts occurred, followed by Laura and Nathan thanking everyone for their attendance, support, and prayers. After dinner, guests were treated to the recently cut cake and everyone was encouraged to check out the hundreds of cookies distributed throughout the hall and take a bag home with them. In true Italian tradition, family members and friends had baked cookies for the reception. It was by far the most diverse and greatest number of cookies we had ever seen at a wedding. The newlyweds were serenaded by the wedding party to the song "Kiss the Girl" from the Little Mermaid—a tune perfect for the moment. Song and dance continued well into the evening.

By all accounts, Joe Brammeier had truly outdone himself with a Las Vegas-style show that gave people something to talk about for a long time. He satisfied the definition of epic and delivered the perfect wedding gift to his sister.

Laura's appointment on September 1 with Dr. Uhm

was extremely positive. The MRI demonstrated no evidence of residual or recurrent tumor, her ECOG performance score was 0, and she had returned to work shortly after the wedding. Laura started the six-cycle maintenance dose of Temozolomide.

After receiving good news from the visit to Mayo, Laura and Nathan decided to take a honeymoon trip to Destin, Florida, in October. The original plan was to travel to Mexico, but still dealing with the uncertainty of Laura's condition, staying in the states seemed to be more sensible. They had been through a lot. The time was right for the two of them to get away.

They went to restaurants, spent time at the beach, and took long walks. They welcomed the opportunity to forget about everything and simply enjoy each other. The trip did them both wonders physically, emotionally, and spiritually.

Wanting to get back into the social scene and knowing winter was not too far off, Laura and Nathan scheduled a long weekend trip to Anaheim, California, to see Paul participate in UFC Fight Night on Fox scheduled for November 12. This was the first UFC mixed martial arts event televised by Fox. The main event was the heavyweight championship with Paul fighting on the undercard. Paul unfortunately lost his match on a split decision. They attended the after party and had fun mingling with the fighters and various celebrities.

They appreciated the warm weather and sites of the west coast.

Laura's subsequent appointment on November 16 with Dr. Uhm proved to be equally positive. Laura showed no signs of any side effects other than a mild skin rash associated with the Temozolomide, successfully managed with an antihistamine. The MRI scan continued to show no evidence of tumor, her ECOG performance score was 0, and she had resumed her regular exercise routine.

After eight difficult months, we felt, as they say in Indy racing, we were driving in clean air. Following the trips to Destin and Anaheim, and hearing the encouraging report from Dr. Uhm, Laura and Nathan looked forward to the fast-approaching holiday season.

Even though 2011 was our year to return to Pennsylvania for Thanksgiving or Christmas, it just seemed right for Laura to be with her family. She enjoyed being around her family during the holidays. The Brammeiers invited Donna and I to their home for the holidays. We were welcomed with open arms and appreciated being included in Laura and Nathan's first holiday season as husband and wife.

Laura was especially fond of Christmas. She enjoyed giving and receiving gifts. She neither disappointed nor was disappointed. With the holidays in the books, on to 2012, to see what would lie ahead for the newly wedded couple.

Laura continued to see Dr. Sandre on a monthly basis. All of Dr. Sandre's notes on Laura were sent to Dr. Uhm in a timely manner. At each appointment, Dr. Sandre would inquire as to how Laura was feeling, perform an examination, monitor her vitals, and order bloodwork for a more comprehensive evaluation of Laura's health. At each visit, Laura's ECOG performance score continued to be 0, supported by Laura confirming she had not noticed any issues that could be related to her brain cancer diagnosis. Laura would complete her sixth and final cycle of Temozolomide shortly before her appointment with Dr. Uhm on February 17, 2012. Laura had great faith and respect for Dr. Sandre, a physician who cared very much about Laura.

Fighting, Living, Friendship

Laura was doing terrific. She showed no signs of impairment and continued to work as a personal trainer. Everyone used this to gauge Laura's overall health and felt the trip to Mayo would be a continuation of good reports. Laura had the usual and customary MRI prior to her February 17 appointment with Dr. Uhm. The report came back showing a small focal area of enhancement in the superior (upper) aspect of the surgical cavity. Dr. Uhm provided two possible explanations.

It could be a delayed radiation-associated injury, not an uncommon finding after radiation therapy, or worst-case scenario, a reoccurrence of the tumor. In either case, there was no reason to continue chemotherapy. To help determine the cause of this new development, a repeat MRI would be performed in advance of the next appointment scheduled for March 21. Laura would also see Dr. Parney during that visit. Laura's ECOG performance score continued to be 0. Dr. Uhm's notes referred to the appointment as "a difficult and sad discussion."

The next four weeks seemed to take much longer. It's that way when dealing with uncertainty. Dr. Uhm appeared subdued when he informed Laura and Nathan of the progression of the focal area during the March 21 appointment. He felt they were dealing with tumor rather than radiation injury. Dr. Parney agreed. They were presented with three treatment options: monitor with serial MRIs, try a different chemotherapy agent, or return to the operating room for a second surgical resection. Drs. Parney and Uhm both recommended the surgical option as it would provide more definitive information about the nature of the changes seen on Laura's most recent MRIs. This time, Dr. Parney explained in much greater detail the risks of the surgery, including bleeding, infection, wound-healing difficulties, temporary or permanent neurological worsening, seizures, speech difficulties, paralysis, coma, and death. Hearing these possibilities raised the stakes in going the surgical route. Laura and Nathan agreed to the second surgery.

They were a little alarmed at Dr. Parney's scheduling

of the surgery for March 23. In less than forty-eight hours, Laura would have another brain surgery. It had been just over a year since Laura experienced the initial event. With Laura doing so well and life returning to normal, hearing the tumor was back didn't seem possible. The news caught everyone by surprise.

The findings from the March 21 appointments set in motion a sequence of events that would demonstrate Laura's fight to live and change their lives forever. The following summarizes, in chronological order, Laura's medical treatments and the couple's life events over the next sixteen months.

March 23: Dr. Parney performed a second craniotomy with tumor resection at St. Mary's Hospital. Laura was admitted the day of the surgery and discharged on March 25. The intraoperative and immediate postoperative course were uncomplicated. Laura was not permitted to lift anything over ten pounds for six weeks.

April 9: Appointment with Dr. Uhm who shares the pathology report. A grade III astrocytoma. Laura's ECOG performance score was 0. Dr. Uhm felt there would almost certainly be microscopic tumor around the surgical cavity. He recommended Laura start Lomustine, one of the oldest chemotherapy medications on the market and well known for the treatment of malignant tumors. Lomustine is administered orally once every six weeks. The dosage is based on mg/m2 (a measurement of surface density). Complications associated with Lomustine include bone marrow suppression, infection, and nausea.

May 25: Appointment with Dr. Uhm. Laura tolerated the first cycle of Lomustine. Follow-up MRI showed evidence of tumor progression with a nodular area of enhancement medial to the surgical cavity with evidence of increased edema. ECOG performance score was 0. Laura's chemotherapy was changed to Bevacizumab, a recombinant humanized monoclonal IgG1 antibody that recognizes and attaches to specific proteins (receptors) that are present on the surface of cancer cells. Once attached, it triggers the immune system to attack the cancer cells, which then destroy themselves. Laura received the first infusion prior to going home. Follow-up infusions were scheduled with Dr. Sandre in Des Moines on a biweekly basis.

Nathan's cousin planned his wedding for June 9 in the Philadelphia area. With Laura permitted to fly, it was nice for the four of us to get away for a long weekend. I remember sitting next to Laura at the reception as guests were dancing. I put my arm around her, gave her a kiss on the side of her head, and told her how fortunate Donna and I were to have her as our daughter-in-law. She smiled, a tear fell from her cheek.

Laura had never been to Washington D.C. The following

day we drove the rental car to the nation's capital, checked into our hotel, and ate pizza from a local restaurant, al fresco. It was a beautiful evening to see the lights of the Center City from across the Potomac. The next day we headed to Center City and began a walking tour on our own. I had been to D.C. many times and was familiar with the landscape and location of the monuments. We spent the morning hours near the White House so we would be close to the Old Ebbitt Grill, established in 1856 as the oldest dining saloon in Washington D.C. We had reservations for lunch.

After lunch, we headed to see the monuments, the National Mall, and made a final stop at Arlington National Cemetery. We did have to deal with one issue. That weekend was the 100th anniversary of the Girl Scouts. There were tens of thousands of them running around. We all agreed to never buy a box of Girl Scout cookies again.

I was glad Laura had the chance to see those iconic symbols of the United States. Laura was exhausted from the weekend. The next day we checked out and headed to the airport to return home.

July 9: Appointment with Dr. Uhm. Laura was tolerating the Bevacizumab infusions and continued personal training with no limitations. The MRI showed further tumor progression despite Laura's excellent clinical status and ECOG performance score of 0. Dr. Uhm would consult with Dr. Parney to see if Laura would be a candidate to participate in a clinical study, a two-stage surgery involving infusion of an oncologic measles virus into the tumor followed by a return to the operating room in five days for tumor resection.

July 18: Appointment with Dr. Parney. He confirmed progression of tumor. The tumor measured 3 cm in diameter with surrounding swelling. For the third time, three options were presented to Laura and Nathan. The first was observation with serial MRIs. With this option Laura would become symptomatic in weeks and die within a matter of a few months. The second option was a third craniotomy with tumor resection. The third option was resection and participation in the experimental oncolytic measles virus study. Laura would need to qualify for the experimental option and be off the Bevacizumab for at least four weeks prior to infusion of the measles virus.

During the screening process, an abnormality in Laura's bloodwork disqualified her from the measles study. Once again, hopes for this new treatment vanished and they were left with Laura undergoing a third surgery and switching to another chemotherapy agent.

July 27: Dr. Parney performed a third craniotomy with tumor resection. As with the other surgeries, all immediate family members were in Rochester. Dr. Parney did not identify any intraoperative issues and continued to be cautiously positive at the post-surgical debriefing. I did speak to him in private commenting on his continued, albeit guarded, optimism versus Laura's eventual fate. I remember Dr. Parney telling me, "You can never take away hope." I could understand that feeling in his line of work. It showed me the humanistic side to Dr. Parney and furthered my confidence in him. So, in addition to prayer, hope became part of Laura's treatment. The MRI taken the next day once again did not demonstrate tumor. Laura was discharged on July 29 with similar restrictions for previous surgeries.

August 7: Appointment with Dr. Uhm. Laura reported occasional speech difficulties. ECOG performance score was 0. Laura wanted to get back to exercising. The pathology report identified the tumor had advanced to a grade IV glioma, a glioblastoma. The MRI did not show evidence of tumor. Due to the tumor returning while Laura was on Bevacizumab, Dr. Uhm changed her chemotherapy to high-dose Procarbazine, following a 28-day on, 28-day off regimen. Procarbazine is an alkylating agent. The exact mechanism of antineoplastic action is unknown but is thought to inhibit DNA, RNA, and protein synthesis. A second round of radiation therapy was still an option if chemotherapy failed to arrest tumor reoccurrence.

Over the previous fifteen months, Laura had three major brain surgeries, multiple courses of different chemotherapy agents, and one round of radiation therapy. Her physical strength and mental fortitude were amazing. Nathan's devotion to Laura was unwavering. He tried to give her as normal a life as possible. He was her pillar of strength.

Eighteen days after the third craniotomy, they celebrated their first anniversary. Laura had not returned to Wilton in a while so she and Nathan celebrated with the Brammeiers the weekend before their anniversary. Later, Donna and I took Laura and Nathan out for a quiet, relaxing dinner. It was nice, just the four of us, putting all they had dealt with on the sideline if just for a few hours.

The cover of a card Laura gave to Nathan on their anniversary read, "To my husband, my best friend, my partner in life." Inside she wrote:

> *You are the best husband ever! We have been through so much and if you weren't my best friend, it would have been hard. You made me smile and laugh on a bad day. You are the first person I think about when something good happens You are the person I want to share everything with. Thanks for all my memories. Good, great, happy, and sad. I am so fortunate to share my past, present, and future with someone so perfect for me. I love you.*
>
> *Laura*

After Laura's third brain surgery, the best opportunity for Laura and Nathan to have a child would be through a surrogate, should Laura be unable to carry. Laura had previously mentioned the idea of surrogacy to Kara during the IVF process resulting in the embryos.

A subsequent conversation with Kara in the presence of Nathan occurred in August. It was Kara who asked the question, "Why are you looking for a surrogate?" Her follow-up comment caught both Laura and Nathan by surprise. Kara told them, "I was planning on doing this and have been going to my obstetrician preparing for this since you first brought it up. Let's do this." It was the greatest gift Kara could give her best friend of twenty-four years.

Kara made the offer before she brought her husband, Aaron, into the conversation. IVF and surrogacy had been around for some time. If you are not familiar with the concept, it may be difficult to understand why someone would volunteer to carry someone else's child. After Kara spoke to Aaron about the process and procedure, he voiced his full support of the decision. Aaron understood the relationship between Kara and Laura. It was a truly remarkable commitment and sacrifice on the part of Kara and Aaron.

Frozen Embryo Transfer (FET) is a complex process involving the science of the human female body, medications, and timing. In the case of a surrogate, preparation begins four to six weeks in advance of the embryo transfer. This requires several medications taken at prescribed times synchronized with the surrogate's cycle. The overall goal is to prepare the uterine lining (endometrium) to receive the transferred embryos and promote development into a healthy live birth.

Embryo transfer is an office-based procedure that does not require anesthesia. It takes approximately thirty minutes. After the procedure, the surrogate is encouraged to rest for the remainder of the day. The next day, except for vigorous activities, life goes on and daily activities such as walking, driving, and working can resume provided they do not require significant physical effort. The physician provides instructions on the dos and don'ts.

The Centers for Disease Control website provides success rates for fertility clinics in all states. Data includes the percent of successful FETs that result in healthy live births. On average, this is between fifty to sixty percent.

Appointments were scheduled with Laura's fertility physician and Kara's obstetrician. The fertility office coordinated the visits and both offices exchanged medical information to expedite the transfer. The process also required both parties signing legal documents identifying the role of each party and legal guardianship of any child born. Kara worked directly with Laura's fertility team to prepare for embryo implantation.

September 17: Appointment with Dr. Uhm. Laura tolerated the Procarbazine without any ill effects. She was experiencing occasional word-finding difficulties, but otherwise she had a normal neurological examination. Sadly, the MRI scan showed tumor progression. Laura would begin radiation therapy to be administered in the Radiation Oncology Department of Mayo.

September 25–October 8: Laura received fractionated radiation therapy during the weekdays, taking the weekends to recover. Fractionated radiation therapy divides the radiation dose into ten sessions over a two-week period. This required Laura to stay in Rochester during the week. Lenore, Donna, and Nathan divided the time to stay with Laura while away from home. She tolerated the sessions well. Patients typically "ring the bell" after completing the final session, but in an act of defiance Laura bypassed the bell and quickly exited the building.

A week after Laura completed the radiation therapy, Kara traveled to Des Moines for the transfer procedure. The transfer of two embryos went well. Kara stayed overnight with Laura and Nathan to rest for the trip home the next day. They awaited the results of a pregnancy test to be performed in two weeks.

Ten days after the procedure, Kara indicated she had not experienced any changes in terms of her body's response to the transfer compared to her two previous pregnancies. Surrogates tend to experience changes consistent with pregnancy around the eight-day mark.

A few days later, Kara notified Laura and Nathan the procedure was unsuccessful. As you can imagine, everyone was heartbroken and disappointed, especially Kara. That disappointment was short-lived. Not to be deterred, Kara expressed her commitment to a second attempt as soon as possible.

October 31: Appointment with Dr. Uhm. Laura was experiencing some speech difficulties that were more noticeable at the end of the day. She complained of an occasional mild headache. Neurologic testing was normal. The MRI showed significant radiographic progression of contrast enhancement seen in the surgical cavity and extensive edema encompassing a substantial portion of the left hemisphere. The radiologist and Dr. Uhm were unable to determine the contribution radiation therapy made to the increase in edema. Dr. Uhm reinstated Bevacizumab. Laura received an initial dose that day, to be followed by a second dose in two weeks, then every three weeks.

That second embryo transfer attempt began in early November but was cancelled toward the end of the preparation phase due to a lack of synchronization of the transfer with Kara's cycle. After further investigation, the fertility physician determined Kara's estrogen levels were the problem. This could be addressed should Kara wish to proceed with another attempt. Without hesitation, Kara confirmed her readiness to give Laura and Nathan a child. This would occur after the 2012–2013 winter holiday season.

The Brammeiers prepared a feast for the Thanksgiving holiday. Many of Laura's extended family were in attendance. Not knowing the plans for Christmas, which would be determined by the outcome of the next visit to Mayo, Laura and Nathan decided to make it a long weekend with Laura's family. Donna and I made Thanksgiving a one-day trip to Wilton. There is always something to be thankful for. We still had Laura.

December 6: Appointment with Dr. Uhm. Laura was no longer experiencing headaches. She was doing well with no limitations. A full neurologic exam was normal. The MRI identified tremendous radiographic improvement in terms of the size of the lesion but also of the surrounding edema. She would continue the Bevacizumab every three weeks with the schedule coordinated by Dr. Sandre. Finally, good news going into the upcoming holidays. Dr. Uhm even agreed to take a photo with Laura and Nathan. A photo they proudly posted on Nathan's Facebook page.

Donna, Nathan, and I had not returned to visit Donna's family over Christmas for several years. With Laura's good report and no travel restrictions, we decided to return to Pennsylvania for Christmas. To break up the travel, we stayed at Lenore and Doug's home the first night. This decreased our travel time by several hours and gave Laura and Nathan the chance to see and exchange gifts with her family. The next day we made the ten-hour trip to Butler, taking many breaks along the way. Donna has a big family and they were all anxious to see Laura and Nathan.

The couple never looked better. They were overwhelmed by the love from Donna's family, the well wishes, and gifts. As much as the couple just wanted to blend in, they were the focus of everyone's attention. We headed home to enjoy a much quieter New Year's holiday.

January 11: Appointment with Dr. Uhm. Laura's last dose of Bevacizumab was December 28. Laura noted mild word-finding difficulties; otherwise, neurologic testing was normal. The MRI showed further radiographic improvement with continued reduction in contrast enhancement and size of the hyperintensity (edema) in the left hemisphere. The Bevacizumab was discontinued and her treatment shifted to observational mode. This was the news everyone had hoped for.

February 12: Appointment with Dr. Uhm. Laura was doing well. She continued to go to the gym with no limitations. Neurologic exam was normal. The MRI showed the possible presence of tumor. Areas of contrast enhancement had increased in size and intensity. The changes could still be related to radiation therapy. Bevacizumab was reinstated with first dose given at the end of the appointment. Subsequent doses would be administered by every three weeks. If the next scan showed radiographic improvement, chemotherapy would be continued for an additional two or three doses.

Everyone remained optimistic. That was the only choice. We all knew what was at stake with the March 25 appointment.

In February, Kara began to prepare for the next attempt as a surrogate for Laura and Nathan. Laura had responded well to the second round of radiation therapy. Kara's estrogen levels were adjusted and all systems were a go. In early March, she traveled to Des Moines for the embryo transfer procedure. For the second time, two embryos were transferred without complication. As with the initial transfer, Kara stayed with Laura and Nathan overnight then returned home. After a few days of limited activities, Kara returned to her normal daily routine. We could only hope and pray for a positive result.

After a week, Kara reported experiencing a feeling like her previous pregnancies. At two weeks, Kara's pregnancy test came back positive. The first ultrasound on March 18 identified the presence of two embryos, one slightly larger than the other. Due to the size difference, the obstetrician cautioned on the possibility of the smaller one failing to develop. Nonetheless, spirits were high. The possibly of twins only increased everyone's enthusiasm. An excited Laura and Nathan shared the news with Laura's parents. Nathan handed us a card created in the likeness of the Dr. Seuss book, *The Cat in the Hat*, with the introduction of Thing One and Thing Two.

March 25: Appointment with Dr. Uhm. Although Laura was doing well clinically, her MRI revealed significant progression of the disease, referred to as tumor burden. Dr. Uhm had always been upfront with Laura and Nathan. He expressed his disappointment in the situation and let them know there were limited treatment options available. For the first time, he brought up the idea of transitioning to palliative care.

Dr. Uhm closed his medical note with, "This was very sad news for Laura and her family." The news that day can only be described as devastating and triggered Nathan's search for a clinical trial that would extend Laura's life. They had to juggle the emotions of Laura's health and knowing their wish to be parents appeared to be a reality. They outwardly remained positive and optimistic.

After informing Dr. Uhm about Kara, Nathan asked Dr.

Uhm to help him identity a clinical trial for Laura. At that time, the Mayo Clinic did have a Phase I clinical study but the wait list was long and she was unlikely to meet the study-qualifying criteria. Dr. Uhm agreed to reach out to a colleague at Duke University Medical Center while at the same time Nathan made the commitment to leave no stone unturned.

The process of finding a clinical trial is extraordinarily time consuming, challenging, and exhausting. Initial contacts need to be made with variable responses, including no response.

Medical records need to be repeatedly signed off on and sent. If you are fortunate, you find an institution that offers a clinical trial. That's just the beginning, as each subject is vetted by way of a comprehensive review of the patient's medical record to determine if they qualify for the trial.

At the same time, you come to appreciate everyone working toward a common goal: to keep Laura alive. It involves a coordinated effort from your medical team, family, and friends creating a network through personal connections—and doing so, knowing you are working against time.

After the March 25 appointment, Dr. Uhm sent a cover letter and Laura's medical records to Duke University Medical Center requesting assistance to determine possible treatment opportunities, including a clinical trial. Dr. Uhm had a connection at Duke and Nathan had family in North Carolina who could assist with travel and lodging. Shortly thereafter, Dr. Uhm learned there were no trial opportunities available at Duke for which Laura would meet the enrollment requirements.

In early April, Nathan learned of a clinical trial at Rush University Medical Center in Chicago. Laura's information was sent to the Director of the Coleman Foundation Comprehensive Brain Tumor Center. Spirits were lifted when Laura was scheduled for an appointment on April 19, 2013. Several options were presented to Laura and Nathan during the visit. Rush had a Phase I clinical trial using Picropodophyllin, a chemical found in the mayapple plant. Picropodophyllin acts as an inhibitor of the insulin-like growth factor 1 receptor, having potential anti-cancer activity and potent activity in the suppression of tumor cell proliferation and induction of tumor cell death. This was combined with a surgical procedure. A second option involved a non-chemotherapy agent approved by the FDA but had not been used to treat brain cancer.

Even though it would require weekly visits and monthly imaging, Laura and Nathan preferred the Phase I clinical trial that included surgery. They were provided a copy of the informed consent document to review and were scheduled to return for further evaluation. Laura had cleared the criteria during this prequalifying appointment. A week later, they returned to Rush University Medical Center for the next step in the process. They returned to Iowa, disappointed after being informed the clinical trial had been suspended due to adverse reactions in participants.

Four weeks after Kara's initial ultrasound, a follow-up study identified only one fetus. Kara's physician performed the ultrasound due to concerns over having difficulty detecting any heartbeats. The study did reveal the remaining fetus had a strong heartbeat. All other developmental measures were normal. They were saddened over the loss but their hopes continued for the remaining fetus.

After the setback from Rush University and the update on Kara, Nathan decided it was time for the two of them to get away and regroup. They needed to temporarily set aside what was happening and just be with each other, without outside interference. It was time to head to Las Vegas. Nathan posted a photo on Facebook: the two of them in front of the Bellagio. You could see in their faces the toll the past two years had taken on both of them. You could also see how much they cared for each other.

Other opportunities at The Cleveland Clinic in Cleveland and Allegheny Health in Pittsburgh that initially appeared promising quickly disappeared after

Laura was rejected following review of her medical record. Several other highly respected medical centers were contacted but had nothing available for Laura.

Laura and Nathan communicated regularly with Kara to check on her condition. Kara continued to see her obstetrician on a regular basis in what would be considered a normal pregnancy. Kara did experience more nausea in the first trimester compared to her previous pregnancies. This appeared to be a consequence of adjusting estrogen levels in preparation for the transfer that continued into the first trimester.

In May, Nathan's uncle Aaron became aware of a clinical trial at MD Anderson Cancer Center in Houston, Texas. Laura appeared to meet the baseline qualifying criteria. Mayo sent her medical record on May 14. The Center quickly responded to the request for consultation with an appointment scheduled for May 21. As Laura's family grew anxious over her treatment status, I submitted the following communication to her parents and siblings on May 17:

> *I want to provide an update on what we know about Laura and her treatment. Laura's condition has progressed to the glioblastoma stage. As you know, this is a very serious condition. I am sure you have at some point searched the internet on this disease. If you have not, I would encourage you to do so to fully understand her situation.*

Unfortunately, Laura has not responded long-term to the previous conventional treatments (surgery, radiation, and chemotherapy). I have taken the time to review her medical record.

Laura's name was placed on a wait list for a clinical trial at Mayo. There have been no openings to date. Her most recent treatment has been resulting in a less than hoped for effect on the tumor. Many of the clinical trials involve surgery. Any clinical trial involving surgery requires the subject to be off chemotherapy for a minimum of four weeks. After the Rush University clinical trial was suspended, many of us and most of all Nathan worked feverishly to identify other opportunities for Laura. Many of the clinical trials would not accept Laura as her previous treatments and reoccurrence excluded her from the study, which have very defined criteria for acceptance and governmental oversight.

Another promising clinical trial involving surgery at the Cleveland Clinic fell through Wednesday. This is the frustration in dealing with clinical trials. Nathan's uncle (Aaron) identified a clinical trial at MD Anderson Cancer Center in Houston. This is a very reputable medical institution. My brother has connections in Houston and has made a few calls seeking out assistance if needed. We are attempting to contact MD Anderson to see if Laura can receive a dose of Bevacizumab prior to going to Houston this Tuesday. If she is not permitted to have the dose and does not qualify for the trial, she will once again be administered Bevacizumab. I have made flight arrangements for Laura, Nathan and Lenore.

Dr. Uhm continues to try and identify options for Laura but they are limited and time sensitive. For those wondering about a plan, at this point there are no specific guidelines to follow. There is no wrong move. There is not right move. There is only the move made with continued consultation with Drs. Uhm and Sandre. The Mayo people are some of the best in the world as are the people at MD Anderson Cancer Center.

Please let me know if you have any questions concerning this information.

Respectfully,
Tim

Two days before the trip to Houston, Laura was hospitalized in Des Moines with severe pain as a result of increased intracranial pressure associated with growth of the tumor. To control the swelling, Laura received high doses of steroids. Laura's hospitalization lasted three days. After being discharged she was to make an appointment to see Dr. Uhm.

May 23: Appointment with Dr. Uhm. He reinstated the administration of Bevacizumab and she was to continue on the oral steroids. Laura was no longer able to travel by air or drive long distances. This would be the final time they would see each other.

Throughout this process, Nathan did everything in his power to find treatments for Laura, even reaching out to domestic and international biotechnology companies. I recall a conversation with Nathan following the final appointment at Mayo when he confided in me not knowing what to do. With tears in our eyes, I told him how proud I was of him and all that he had done. The time had come to rely on prayer and keeping Laura comfortable, all the while her medical team continued to treat her with conventional brain cancer therapy and steroids to control the swelling.

Even as her health continued to decline, Laura insisted on attending two events. The first was at the Navy Pier in Chicago the weekend of May 31–June 2. Nathan and five other members of CrossFit 515 qualified for the CrossFit Games North Central Regional. The team finished third and qualified for the CrossFit Games in California, the Super Bowl of fitness, scheduled in mid-July. Laura did not miss a minute of the competition. You could see Laura's excitement every time Nathan was on the floor competing. It would be the last time she would travel out of state. Nathan would miss the 2013 CrossFit Games.

Laura's sister Katy and her fiancée Scot planned their wedding for June 22. In early June, Laura's speech continued to be affected and she began to experience right-side weakness with loss of muscle mass. She developed a drop foot condition on her right side. Drop foot occurs when the nerve supply to the muscles that enable a person to move their foot upward at the ankle is affected, making it difficult to walk. Laura used a foot ankle brace to help her ambulate. These manifestations of her disease were particularly noticeable at the wedding.

There was some conversation about postponing the wedding. Laura insisted it go on as planned. In her mind, postponing would be a sign of giving up. She was determined to support her younger sister as her Maid of Honor. Nathan was particularly anxious about Laura's role and her ability to fulfill her duties. Laura chose not to wear the brace at the wedding ceremony. We held our breath as the Best Man escorted Laura down the aisle. It took all of Laura's strength, concentration, and will to make that walk. Everyone felt a sense of relieve when the ceremony ended, especially Nathan.

At the reception, when the Maid of Honor and Best Man were introduced, Nathan recognized how Laura struggled to walk at the ceremony, even with assistance. He did as he always did: he intervened to protect her. He carried her through the curtain to her seat. At that moment, the inevitable became a reality unless a new treatment could be found.

The ultrasound scheduled on July 3 would be the big reveal. By the second trimester, Kara's nausea resolved. Unfortunately, Laura's communication skills and physical abilities were in rapid decline. With Nathan at her side, he recorded the session and Laura's reaction when informed they were having a girl. Despite her disabilities, she repeatedly expressed her excitement by saying, "It's a girl; I am so happy."

Laura and Kara had previously talked about names depending on the gender of the child. In a tribute to Kara, whose middle name was Lynn, the baby's first name would be Caralyn. Her middle name would be the same as Laura's, Elizabeth. There were no dissenting opinions.

The time had come for Kara and Aaron to tell their two children, who would soon notice a change in the appearance of their mother. Kara and Aaron sat down with their nine-year-old son and six-year-old daughter to explain in language they could understand to the best of their ability. At least that was the goal.

Their son was most interested in knowing the legality of such an arrangement and asked a few logistical questions. Then he just shrugged it off. Their daughter expressed disappointment the baby would not be a permanent fixture in the family. She did ask if they could keep her for at least one night? She liked to share the story but occasionally forgot to include a few important details, telling people, "My mom is having a baby but it's not my dad's," or "my mom is having a baby but we can't keep it." This required some clarification from Kara.

Laura and Nathan were dealing with the rapid decline in her health while knowing the gender and name of their child who would be born in less than five months.

Hail Mary

In football it's referred to as a Hail Mary, an attempt to score by a long pass in the final seconds of the game. It's considered a desperation play with low odds for a successful outcome but still worth the chance. We had one final attempt to extend Laura's life. Frank had a colleague from work diagnosed with the same condition a few years before Laura. Frank recalled how impressed his colleague was with a particular physician at Duke University. Frank took the initiative to contact the spouse of his colleague. She provided him with the name of the physician.

In a long shot, on July 17, I reached out to the physician, a well-respected neuro-oncologist at the Duke University Cancer Center Brain Tumor Clinic. I explained Laura's condition and left my contact information on a voicemail. I ended my call thinking I would never hear back. Within the hour, I received a return phone call. I provided additional details on Laura's treatments and current condition. The physician mentioned a new combination of chemotherapy agents they were treating patients in similar circumstances as Laura and seeing good results. He did mention the insurance company would initially decline approval but with persistence they would cover the cost. I shared this conversation with Dr. Sandre, who followed up by contacting the physician.

As predicted, the insurance company denied coverage. That did not prohibit administering the medications to Laura, but that would require approval from the medical director of the cancer center. The next step was for Dr. Sandre to gain that approval. Dr. Sandre did not receive a return call. It was our Hail Mary.

The Baby Shower and Cake

With Laura's health deteriorating, the question of a baby shower was discussed shortly after Katy and Scot's wedding. Donna approached Laura about having a shower. Laura confirmed her interest in having a shower. Even though a baby shower is typically held four to six weeks before the birth date, there was a degree of urgency. Everyone recognized that without saying it. A baby shower gave Laura something to look forward too.

To have enough time to send out invitations and plan the shower, the date selected was Saturday, July 20 from 1:00 to 3:00 p.m. This allowed for slightly less than three weeks to make all the arrangements. Out of comfort and convenience for Laura, the shower would be held at their home in Grimes.

Laura and Lenore put together a list of family and friends to invite. Donna supplemented that list with names from Nathan's side of the family. As you might expect, it was a large list.

Donna took the lead in organizing the event. The various duties were distributed. It came as no surprise the number of family members and friends of Laura who volunteered to help. Their offers were appreciated and accepted.

In advance of the shower, Caralyn's nursery had already been painted, alternating horizontal stripes of tan and off-white colors, one foot in height that encircled the room. It matched a room Laura liked in Kara and Aaron's home. Caralyn's crib, dresser, and changing table were arranged as Laura had requested. A rocking chair was positioned in one of the corners. It was a chair Laura and Nathan had given to Donna as a Mother's Day gift for when Caralyn stayed at our house. For now, it remained in Grimes.

The color scheme for the bedding and changing table were pink with small brown polka dots. Butterflies of various dimensions matching the colors of the bedding were hung on the walls. Centered above the crib was a large wooden monogram painted brown with the initials CEY. Caralyn's room was ready to be filled with gifts and love.

THE BABY SHOWER AND CAKE

Laura's family and Kara arrived around 9:00 a.m. The next three hours were dedicated to preparing for the shower. Banners, party favors, and balloons decorated the house. Laura was quiet but excited. She had difficulty moving around so she would be positioned in the center of the sofa with Kara and another friend, to be determined, sitting beside her. Shortly before the start of the shower, food, drink, and the cake were placed out for the guests to indulge. At the same time, the men were shuffled off to a local tavern for lunch. Nathan would periodically text Donna to check in on Laura.

Considering the time frame and circumstances, no one kept a close eye on the RSVPs. It was assumed many family members, relatives, and friends would attend. That would be an understatement. Nearly eighty people were located throughout the house. With such a high number of guests, sticking to the schedule of activities became difficult. It pretty much came down to people helping themselves to food, beverages, and cake.

From a nutritional perspective, Laura avoided consuming sugar. Her anti-sugar position only intensified after her cancer diagnosis. Studies do not necessarily directly link sugar to cancer. However, sugar is associated with obesity, which is linked to many forms of cancer.

Regardless, Laura steered clear of sugar. During the shower, Kara encouraged Laura to have a piece of her cake. Laura initially declined the offer. Kara, not to be outdone by her best friend, repeated the request. Their eyes met for a brief moment. Laura agreed to have a piece.

She consumed the cake in a matter of minutes. She smiled at her best friend. Although they never talked about it, Kara sensed by Laura eating the cake, she understood the gravity of her situation.

There were two main areas where people congregated. The family room where Laura opened the gifts with Kara by her side and Caralyn's nursery. It was in Caralyn's nursery where questions and comments about Laura's health occurred on a frequent basis, all in a caring and respectful manner. Away from Laura, many shed tears as they tried to balance Laura's condition against the joy of a new life just four months away.

Many of Laura's friends and relatives had not seen Laura over the past several months. Some were caught off guard and a few shaken by her appearance, with now-obvious disabilities as a result of her disease. This became apparent when Laura tried to stand and walk her own. She did not have the strength or coordination to manage a small flight of stairs. Donna witnessed Laura attempting to negotiate the stairs and quickly intervened, providing the help she needed. It was a troubling sight to see from someone they knew as the poster person for health and fitness.

THE BABY SHOWER AND CAKE

As the shower ended, the difficult position relatives and friends found themselves in was knowing this might be the last time they saw Laura. Guests that focused on Caralyn did much better than those who directed their attention on Laura. It was an overwhelming and emotional experience for everyone in attendance. One person stood out as showing the most strength: Laura. She refused to allow sadness to be part of the day or her life.

After the guests left, the men were contacted and returned to help with the clean-up. Nathan was the first to greet Laura. You could appreciate his relief in seeing her. The gifts were moved to Caralyn's nursery. Clothing items were neatly stacked close to the rocking chair where Laura could see them and hold them should she choose. The larger boxed items requiring assembly were placed in another area of the nursery. I left to take my brother, in for the weekend, to the airport on his return to North Carolina.

Donna was the last to leave. She insisted on that. Everything needed to be organized and every room spotless to make life easier for Laura and Nathan. She left them sitting side-by side. They hugged and thanked her—our prince and princess.

Laura was completely drained, but happy she had participated in an event all expecting mothers should experience: their baby's shower.

Nathan as a member of the Milwaukee Brewers minor league baseball team the West Virginia Power in 2006 (photo courtesy of Robin Black).

Laura, including Kara, and her close friends from St. Ambrose University (photo courtesy of Shirk Photography).

Engagement day photograph of Laura and Nathan in November 2010 (photo courtesy of BobbiJo Wolfe).

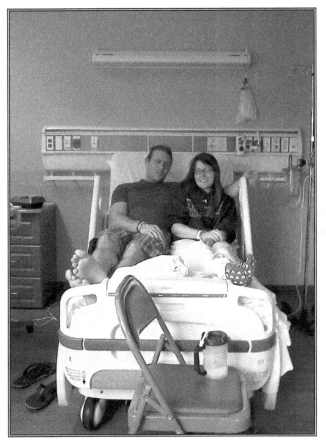

Laura and Nathan preparing for discharge from St. Mary's Hospital in Rochester following her surgery in May 2011.

Wedding day portrait of Laura and Nathan photographed in downtown Wilton (photo courtesy of Shirk Photography).

Laura and Nathan wearing "I Love Laura" t-shirts at the fundraiser held by The Blazing Saddle in Des Moines' East Village.

Laura and Nathan on their honeymoon in Destin, Florida.

Entrance to Nathan's gym CrossFit Merle Hay in Des Moines.

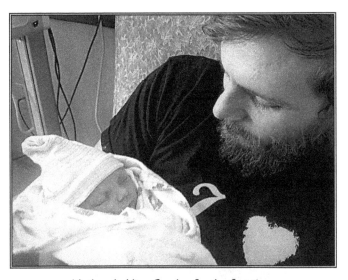

Nathan holding Caralyn for the first time.

Nathan and Caralyn together out for dinner on a date night.

End of Life

On Sunday, Laura had Nathan assemble the various baby toys, bouncers, and rockers received the day before. They had a quiet and peaceful Sunday. It would be the final time just the two of them would be together in their home.

In dealing with advanced brain cancer, circumstances can change rapidly, and they did. Nathan called Donna Monday morning and let her know Laura was sleeping late and he had difficulty waking her. Donna drove to the house to find Nathan was able to rouse Laura out of bed and helped dressed her for the day. Laura seemed off, not wanting to engage much in conversation or activity. As the day progressed, Laura began to complain of a headache. A call to her physician yielded a recommendation to increase the steroid dosage to control the intracranial pressure. The dose was increased as suggested. Late Monday afternoon, based on Laura's demeanor, as her pain continued to increase her capacity to communicate and function diminished. She needed to go to the hospital. I called Laura's parents to provide an update. Nathan drove Laura to the emergency department at the medical center where she had been previously hospitalized. They were accompanied by Donna, sitting in the back seat with Laura. I followed in my car. Donna later recalled seeing Laura hit her fist against the seat as a sign of the severity of her pain.

When we arrived at the emergency department, it did not appear to be overly busy from the perspective of the waiting area. I described Laura's condition to the front desk person and stressed the level of pain she was experiencing. The intake nurse completed her evaluation after being checked in. It took Lenore just over two hours to reach the hospital. During that time, I repeatedly requested that Laura's pain be managed. Each time I was informed they were busy and would get to Laura as soon as possible.

Over two hours had passed before Laura was triaged to a hallway bed in the emergency department. The department seemed busy, but from my observation, many of the conditions appeared to be non-life-threatening in nature. I cornered a nurse and requested that Laura be administered medications to control her pain and the underlying cause, intracranial pressure. I offered my willingness to speak to a physician if she was unable to help Laura. The nurse mentioned the emergency department and pharmacy needed to follow a protocol for pain medicine. I can appreciate protocols but not at the expense of a person with a terminal condition experiencing intractable pain.

After three hours of waiting, Laura was seen by one of the emergency department physicians. At that point, Laura could not verbally communicate her symptoms. I reviewed her medical history with the physician. The physician finally ordered a pain medication that continued to be delayed due to communication issues between departments. Once the physician completed his examination, he pulled the family aside and informed us of Laura's dire condition. He advised consultation with hospice.

I would later send the following letter to the Chief Executive Officer of the medical center:

> *October, 15, 2013*
> *Dear Sir,*
>
> *I chose to wait for a period of time before sending this letter. My daughter-in-law Laura Yoho was seen in the emergency department on July 22, 2013. She arrived between 7:00–7:30 p.m.,*

transported by her husband, Nathan. After the initial assessment by the intake nurse, she sat in the waiting area for two hours. I was clear that due to Laura's advanced brain tumor she was unable to communicate her concerns and was experiencing significant pain. After two hours she was placed on a bed in the hallway of the emergency department and continued to wait. We asked that she be given something for pain. We were informed Laura needed to wait until she was seen by a physician. She was finally evaluated by a physician, in the hallway, who informed us in a professional manner that Laura was dying. The physician ordered the pain medication but she continued to wait even with our continued requests to manage her pain. We were told the holdup was the pharmacy. I am not sure if this was related to policy or staffing. Regardless, it was terribly unfortunate. All the providers seemed like caring people but for some reason there was a breakdown in recognizing the urgency of Laura's condition. Laura died the next day. Laura's experience that evening was extremely disappointing. I hope this letter will prevent others from having a similar experience.

Very Respectfully,
Tim Yoho

I promptly received a response from the administration, offering condolences and acknowledging the delay in managing Laura's pain. I was assured the institution's pain protocols would be reviewed to ensure they facilitated treatment without undue delay. I appreciated the response.

We did not know what to expect when representatives from the hospice team came to meet Laura and family members after the physician finished meeting with us. Everyone was pleasant and expressed their compassion for Laura's circumstances. A delicate moment occurred when the team leader began talking about the process in the presence of Laura. She would have been able to hear the discussion. I advised the conversation be moved away from Laura.

When presented the option to transport Laura to the hospice center or take her home, Nathan was adamant: she was going home. I found a twenty-four hour pharmacy to fill a prescription for morphine to manage Laura's pain. The hospice team planned to arrive Tuesday morning. Laura reached her home around 11:30 p.m. Once settled, Donna and I drove to our home. Lenore stayed with Laura and Nathan.

Monday night proved to be a restless time for everyone. At 3:30 a.m., I received a call from Nathan; his demeanor was calm yet concerned. He said Laura was resting comfortably but her breathing pattern had recently changed. He described her breathing as slower with a periodic rattling sound. Nathan added she was not responding to his voice. I explained the changes in breathing that occur as a person's body begins to shut down. My advice to him was to hold her, tell her he loved her, and let her know everything would be all right. Even though she was not responding to him that did not mean she could not hear him. I do not know how we made it through that conversation.

The remainder of the night was dedicated to reflection and prayer. Donna and I drove to Grimes shortly after 7:30 a.m. Doug, Joe, Katy, Kara, and Aaron were in route to Grimes in what would normally take about two and a half hours. It did not take that long. The hospice team arrived at 8:00 a.m. to review the process and services that would be made available to Laura and Nathan. The priority was to keep Laura comfortable. The hospice team departed at 10:00 a.m.

Once everyone arrived, the finality of the situation became reality. Over the next several hours everyone spent time with Laura. Although the emergency room physician and hospice team leader felt it might be a few days to a week, we all approached our time with Laura as if it were the final time.

Donna and I decided to take a break and go home for a few hours. We left Grimes shortly after noon. I received the call from Nathan at 2:15 p.m. His voice was shaky but clear. Laura had died. He was by her side when she took her last breath. I expressed my sorrow and let him know we would be on our way shortly. I informed Donna. She knelt to her knees and began to breakdown. She kept repeating, "I should have been there." I told her, "You were."

Upon our arrival, we expressed our condolences to Lenore, Doug, Joe, and Katy. They had just lost their beautiful daughter and sister. Next was Nathan, who did everything a man could do and more to give Laura the life she deserved under the most difficult circumstances. I do not recall saying anything to him—words did not matter, just the longest, hardest hug a father and mother could give their child. Then there was Kara, Laura's friend since second grade—the person carrying her daughter. Donna and I conveyed our profound sadness on the loss of her best friend and committed to help in any way we could through this difficult time and with the birth of our granddaughter. Doug reached out to his close friend Henry Bentley to inform him of Laura's passing. Henry immediately departed from Wilton for Grimes.

Hospice arrived and prepared Laura's body. Everyone was afforded time to spend with Laura and privately say their goodbyes. She looked at peace.

Henry arrived around 5:30 p.m. He communicated his sorrow to everyone, especially the Brammeiers and Nathan. This man who had arranged hundreds of funerals was visibly shaken by the death of Laura.

The time had come to transport Laura back to her hometown. Nathan requested a final moment with her. After several minutes, he picked her up and gently placed her on the gurney. Nathan and Henry carried Laura down a short flight of steps then outside to the opened vehicle. Not a word was spoken, only tears. It is hard to describe what we had just witnessed other than seeing a man being a devoted husband to the very end.

Henry Bentley would later say this was the most difficult funeral he had ever arranged and caused him to consider getting out of the business. He retired a few years later.

Nathan ended the day by calling Dr. Uhm to inform him that Laura had died. Nathan thanked him for all that he had done. Dr. Uhm expressed his condolences. To this day, they continue to communicate.

Laying Laura to Rest

Much like how quickly Laura's health had declined and she lost her battle, her funeral seemed to go by just as swiftly. Nathan traveled to Wilton the day Laura died. He and Lenore would meet with Henry Bentley on Wednesday to discuss Laura's funeral arrangements. Donna and I would leave for Wilton Wednesday afternoon and stay with Lenore and Doug Wednesday night.

Thursday was spent finalizing arrangements. Thursday afternoon Donna and I checked into a hotel in Muscatine waiting to greet family members as they arrived from out of state.

Everyone convened at the Doug and Lenore's home for a cookout out Thursday evening. The mood was somber, with little conversation—a much different setting compared to when celebrating the life of someone who lived a long and rich life.

The visitation would be held on Friday from 4:00–8:00 p.m. with a second opportunity available one hour before the service. The funeral mass was scheduled for Saturday at 10:30 a.m. Father Bob, the priest who married Laura and Nathan, would perform the service.

Donna and I took Nathan to a clothing store in Iowa City Friday morning. In our haste, we had forgotten to bring Nathan's suit. It did provide an opportunity for the three of us to spend time together. It did us all some good to get away, if only for a few hours. He chose Laura's favorite color, purple, for his dress shirt and tie.

Family members, friends from the past and present, work colleagues, and even strangers who had heard about Laura's story attended the visitation in the sanctuary of St. Mary's Church. It was nonstop people for four hours. Some individuals traveled hours to pay their respects. We were overwhelmed by the expression of compassion. The day was filled with tears, with an occasional light laugh or smile. It was an emotionally charged day.

One thing that stood out at the visitation was the number of people who asked about Kara. As you might expect, considering Kara was in her second trimester and had just lost her best friend, we were cautious in directing people to her. If approached, Kara was her usual friendly self and gracious to people who expressed their condolences and admiration for her willingness to carry Laura and Nathan's baby. Aaron was nearby to serve as a buffer.

Nathan spent much of his time with former teammates from the University of Iowa baseball team who had taken the time to travel to Wilton. They were and remain a tight group. He held up well and offered his appreciation to everyone he met.

On Saturday, family members, Kara, and Aaron arrived at St. Mary's Church around 9:00 a.m. Laura was located in the gathering space outside the sanctuary. There were many new faces who did not make the visitation but were attending the service. They paused for a moment to pay their respects and offer their sympathies to family and Kara.

As 10:30 a.m. approached, each of us had the chance to say our final farewells. Nathan was the last to say goodbye to his wife. They were three weeks shy of celebrating their second anniversary. He leaned over, whispered to her, and gave her a final kiss. It was a heartbreaking moment. Henry Bentley closed the casket.

Henry and his family would send Caralyn a gift on her first Christmas. It was a necklace with a silver ornament bearing Laura's fingerprint. The accompanying card read, "Laura touched our lives on earth for a short time, but she left her fingerprint on our hearts forever." Caralyn reserves the necklace for special days.

Serving as casket bearers were Scot (Katy's husband), Aaron (Kara's husband), Jared (Nathan's cousin), Chris (Brammeier family friend), Nick (Brammeier family friend), and Miller (Nathan's cousin). They followed Father Bob into the sanctuary with Laura's casket. Once they had positioned the casket, Henry and Bev (Henry's wife) rotated the casket. In the process, Bev bumped one of the tall candle stands. As it fell, a hand reached out to catch it and return it to its proper location. It was Nathan who caught the stand.

There were no personal testimonials by family members or friends. That would have been difficult considering how quickly everything had unfolded over the past week. The last thing anyone wanted was to breakdown in the process of honoring Laura with so many other factors in play. Father Bob handled the eulogy and tributes. He delivered a message of Laura's transition into God's hands and hope for peace of mind for Laura's family and friends. Father Bob was aware of the unique circumstances with Kara and Caralyn. He encouraged everyone to help Caralyn understand the strength and courage of her mother.

In advance of the service, Donna and I felt the need to provide a message that captured our thoughts about Laura and Nathan. I emailed Father Bob a short statement that he read during the service:

> *Laura and Nathan were our princess and prince. They were soul mates, best friends, husband and wife—the perfect couple. Laura taught us about extraordinary courage and Nathan taught us about unwavering commitment. So many people have been touched by their story. They lived their wedding vows, "In sickness and in health they loved each other all the days of their lives." Laura was Donna's best friend. She was like a daughter to us and we are forever grateful to Doug, Lenore, and the Brammeier family for sharing her. Donna and I were so fortunate to witness perfection, if only for a short time.*

It was a traditional Catholic funeral service. A brief informal period followed the service to greet individuals who attended the ceremony. I recall seeing Gary and Ryan, the father and one of his two sons representing the family Nathan had lived with when he played summer baseball in Rochester. They now lived in Nashville, Tennessee. Seeing them brought a smile to Nathan's face.

Interment followed at Oakdale Cemetery located about a mile from the church. Attendance was limited to family and close friends. The weather that day reminded us of their wedding day.

Laura was laid to rest near a grove of trees, close to other members of the Brammeier family. To the west a corn field awaited the upcoming harvest season. It would be a remarkable and peaceful scene when the sun set on a beautiful Iowa fall day. Nathan, Caralyn, Donna, and I visit the site every time we are in Wilton.

It was a brief ceremony, ending with the Catholic Rite of Committal, the final act of the community of faith in caring for the body of the deceased. In committing the body to its resting place, the community expresses the hope that much like those who have gone before, the deceased awaits the glory of the resurrection. The Rite of Committal is an expression of the communion that exists between the church on earth and the church in heaven. The deceased ascends with the farewell prayers of the community into the welcoming arms of those who no longer need faith, but see God face-to-face. Nathan placed a white rose on Laura's casket. With that, Laura was laid to rest.

We made our way back to Doug and Lenore's home for a quick lunch. Many of our family members headed home immediately after the lunch. For some the drive would take over ten hours. Others scheduled return flights on Sunday morning. The remaining members of our family in the latter group, Nathan, Donna, and I moved to a different hotel for the final night.

This gave us a chance to spend time with our immediate

family. We valued having them with us. Several cousins close to Nathan's age kept him occupied by sharing stories of growing up together.

On Sunday morning, we waited until all our relatives departed for the airport. Nathan, Donna, and I headed home. Laura was no longer with us. I asked Nathan if he wanted me to stay with him. He declined and thanked me for the offer.

The time had come to grieve and honor Laura's life as we prepared for the birth of Caralyn, whose pending arrival was included in Laura's obituary.

Life After Death

After Laura's death, we were all concerned how this would affect Kara and the pregnancy. Kara is an extraordinarily strong person with an equally extraordinary supportive husband and family. She knew Laura may not be alive when Caralyn was born. Kara had the ability to compartmentalize the tragedy of Laura and mourn her death while having the strength to not let her grief affect the pregnancy. Kara would later acknowledge her motivation to have Caralyn increased after losing her best friend and wanting Nathan to have her child. She just needed to not put too much pressure on herself. Kara was determined to bring Caralyn into the world, as she put it, "To have a piece of Laura with us."

In the final trimester, Caralyn had frequent bouts of

hiccups. She also loved to kick and move around. The hiccups were a bit annoying but Kara enjoyed the movement; she considered it a positive signal of Caralyn's development and good health.

With IVF, the date of fertilization and subsequent transfer to the carrier is known. This provides a fairly accurate prediction of the baby's arrival. Past delivery history, the physical examination, ultrasound, and the baby's weight and size combine with other factors to help determine an optimal date for delivery. With that, Kara's obstetrician scheduled Kara to be induced the morning of Tuesday, November 26.

Knowing the date in advance allowed everyone to make the necessary arrangements to avoid a mad dash to the hospital. It also afforded Nathan time to contact Eric Hansen, a reporter from Channel 8 Des Moines, so that he could travel to Trinity Bettendorf Medical Center to video family members waiting on the delivery of Caralyn and the reaction to her birth. This was to be in follow-up to a story Eric had previously done about Laura's battle against brain cancer.

Nathan trusted Eric's judgment in telling the story in a way that would honor Laura and help Caralyn understand the beauty of her mother's life.

Donna, Nathan, and I traveled to Wilton the evening of November 25. Nathan drove separately with an infant car seat occupying the rear passenger seat of his truck. We stayed with Lenore and Doug. The mood was upbeat but you could tell everyone was a little anxious. Kara and Aaron were at home preparing for an early morning trip to the hospital. Their children stayed with relatives.

Kara and Aaron arrived at the hospital around 5:30 a.m. After completing the admission process, a nurse escorted Kara and Aaron to the maternity area of the hospital. Kara's physician arrived soon after and began the induction process.

Family members arrived at the hospital about 8:00 a.m. It was a chilly morning with light flurries. Later in the day the clouds cleared and the sun shined brightly. We were met by a representative of the hospital and directed to the waiting area. Everyone wore their I Love Laura T-shirt. Eric Hansen and his photojournalist were granted clearance in advance. They arrived at 9:30 a.m. We did not notice them in room.

To pass the time, family members would take walks around the medical center campus, head to the cafeteria, or engage each other in casual conversation in the waiting area. A little before noon, a representative from the obstetrics department invited Lenore and Nathan to the birthing room. As the minutes passed the conversations lessened while fidgeting and foot taping dominated the waiting area.

At 12:45 p.m. Katy received a text message from Lenore announcing that Caralyn had arrived at 12:36 p.m., twenty-five months after she was conceived. It was a natural delivery. Both Caralyn and Kara were doing well. A picture accompanied Lenore's text. It took a few seconds for everyone to let it sink in. The pent-up emotion could now be released by a synchronized cheer followed by tears of joy, hugs, and handshakes. At the same time, you could not help but think of Laura and how much she would have cherished experiencing the birth of her daughter. Doug commented, "We have a part of Laura back with us," a thought many were having. The reaction was captured on video by Eric's team.

An hour later family members were permitted to meet Caralyn for the first time. She weighed 7 pounds, 8 ounces with a length of 21 inches. You could immediately see she had features of both her mother and father. At the same time, we offered our indebtedness to Kara and Aaron for what they had just done.

Nathan's expression was one of pure joy and contentment. As he was holding Caralyn, Nathan told Eric, "She's going to know how hard her mother tried to be here for her and what kind of a person she was." Yes, a part of Laura was back. Not a replacement—her own being with a wonderful story.

It was time for Kara to rest, Nathan to bond with his

daughter, and for all of us to process the miracle of Caralyn.

Two days later, Thanksgiving Day, Kara and Caralyn were released from the hospital. Activities shifted to Joe and Lynn's home in Bettendorf. Kara, Aaron, their two children, Nathan, and Caralyn arrived later in the afternoon. They were greeted with hugs from many family members.

Caralyn was passed around under the nervous watch of Nathan. Although this Thanksgiving Holiday had special meaning for the Brammeiers and the Yohos, Nathan was relieved when it ended.

After most family members had left, I wanted to get a breath of fresh air. I stepped out on Joe and Lynn's front porch. Joe joined me. It was a cool and clear evening. I looked to the southwest; low in the sky I saw a brilliant star. The last time I had witnessed this scene was four months earlier after dropping Nathan off at his home on our return from Laura's funeral. From our deck a bright light in the horizon had caught my eye. At first, I thought it was a plane approaching the Des Moines Airport. But it had remained stationary. I shared the story with Joe. We christened it Laura's star. She was signaling us everything would be fine.

That first night, Donna stayed with Caralyn at Joe and Lynn's house while Nathan and I pulled couch duty.

Donna and I returned home the next day. This gave us the chance to move our essential belongings into Nathan's home and prepare for Caralyn's homecoming. As we drove home on Interstate 80 heading west, we passed Wilton, Laura's hometown, where she had been married and laid to rest. We passed Iowa City, where Nathan had graduated from the University of Iowa and played Big Ten baseball with all those memories, and finally, we passed West Des Moines, Nathan's hometown. We were about to start the next chapter in our lives.

Nathan and Caralyn stayed with Kara, Aaron, and their children for five days. They had talked about doing this before Caralyn was born. It did not seem right to just take Caralyn and leave. Kara deserved the chance to spend time with her best friend's daughter. After all, from this day forward Kara would be known as Caralyn's birth mother. It also gave Kara and Aaron's children the chance to share in the experience and later come to understand the enormity of what their parents had done for others.

After the five days, Nathan and Caralyn said their goodbyes to Kara, Aaron, and their children. I am sure they felt a range of emotions. Nathan and Caralyn were on their way home—a single father and his newborn daughter sharing in a new life together with thoughts of Laura never far away.

Eric Hansen's story, "Grief, loss, and joy," aired on February 4, 2014. The video went viral and was picked up by major news organization worldwide. For their work, Eric and photojournalist Glen Biermann received the highest award from the Society of Professional Journalists, the Sigma Delta Chi Award.

"We're so honored Laura's family trusted us to tell this incredibly emotional story," said Eric. "The Yohos allowed us into their lives for sixteen months, capturing both tears of grief and joy. Even more humbling is how Nathan told us he plans to use our story someday to let little Caralyn learn more about her mom."

Glen added, "I'm incredibly grateful for them allowing us to show such an amazing story of family and friends."

Eric and Glenn went on to receive a Regional Edward R. Murrow Award in the Feature Reporting Category on the same story. In June 2015, Eric was honored with an individual National Edward R. Murrow Award in the Small Market Category.

Eric would go on to produce a video when Caralyn turned one and later when Caralyn started kindergarten. Eric and Nathan have maintained their friendship, conveying a mutual respect for one another.

Compassion and Generosity

When first diagnosed with brain cancer and Laura had undergone her initial surgery, radiation therapy, and chemotherapy, she had received get well cards and calls from relatives, a few clients, and close friends. The families didn't say much about her condition, trying to maintain as normal a life as possible. Besides, Laura was doing so well and had not displayed any noticeable affects from her treatment.

Laura and Nathan knew a lot of people. After Laura's third surgery, word spread quickly about Laura's condition. Family members, friends, and even strangers began to reach out to Laura and Nathan, wanting to help. A popular request that kept coming up was to assist them financially. The cost of Laura's care was in the hundreds of thousands of dollars. Laura's health insurance covered a substantial portion of her medical expenses but they still had a significant debt they were responsible to cover.

At first, Donna and I were reluctant to give our endorsement to fundraising activities. We had the resources to help cover the balance. I remember talking to Frank and a close friend about this. They both offered the same opinion: if people want to help, let them. As much as it will assist Laura and Nathan, it provides an opportunity for people to do something that also gives them a rewarding feeling. With that, we removed any concerns about fundraising activities.

It would be impossible to acknowledge all the individuals and organizations that offered assistance to Laura and Nathan in the many of acts of compassion and generosity. It is however important to share examples of support they received.

Nathan's friend, Tom, knew the owner of The Blazing Saddle, a well-known gay bar in the center of Des Moines' historic East Village. The East Village was one of the original commerce centers of the city but fell on hard times in the seventies and eighties. Through a dedicated effort of city leaders, business owners, and entrepreneurial investment, the East Village is now one of the most thriving and diverse districts, boasting many of the finest shopping, dining, and nightlife activities in Iowa.

The Blazing Saddle frequently held fundraising events for nonprofits and other worthy causes. The owner, Bob, AKA "Mongo," opened the bar in 1983. The motto of the bar is, "Never a cover and always a double," so come on in and enjoy. Mongo, a Vietnam war veteran, is a recognizable figure in the Des Moines community. Tom shared Laura and Nathan's story with Mongo. He was agreeable with having The Blazing Saddle host a fundraising activity. The event called, "Bingo for Laura and Nate," was scheduled for Saturday, September 29, 2012 at 2:00 p.m.

Tom sought out sponsors for several theme gift baskets and other items for a raffle and live auction. People learned of the fundraiser through social media announcements, personal communications, and posters hung throughout the bar and in the front window.

This would be a new experience for all of us. Laura and Nathan wore their I Love Laura T-shirts. As people attending the fundraiser began to arrive, you could sense this was going be a fun time for a terrific cause. Guests mixed in well with the regular Blazing Saddle patrons. Joe Brammeier was in his element when the bartender handed him the microphone to announce the names of the winners of several raffle items and to auction off the baskets and other merchandise donated to the event. He is comically irreverent but means no harm.

You recognize that immediately with Joe. I have no doubt he single-handedly raised funds that far exceeded expectations.

Another interesting activity was bingo. The caller, sitting high atop the bar, introduced the game with a precautionary announcement, "This is not your grandmother's bingo!" You paid a fee for your bingo cards with the proceeds going to the fund. To win, your numbers needed to form specific configurations. Let's leave it at that. Vodka Jell-O shots in a variety of shapes circulated throughout the bar as part of the experience.

The event ended around 6:00 p.m. In those four hours, nearly $8,000 was raised—the largest fundraiser to date held at The Blazing Saddle. What an incredible afternoon. We were so grateful to Mongo, the employees of The Blazing Saddle, Nathan's friend Tom, the LGBTQ community, and all who participated in Bingo for Laura and Nate. I do not think anyone will ever forget the love we witnessed for Laura and Nathan that day.

In late October 2012, Nathan's uncle (Aaron) and his cousin (Lauren), both from Pennsylvania, reached out to me. They wanted to start an online fundraising account to assist Laura and Nathan. They knew of my initial hesitation to endorse fundraising events. I did appreciate them coming to me for my support. It became clear that many people were looking for an opportunity to help the young couple. They established a GiveForward

Account titled "Help Laura Win." A Facebook group, "Show Love for Laura," was created to provide updates on Laura's health and progress with fundraising. The initial goal was $15,000.

Shortly after establishing the giving platform, Eric Hansen, the reporter from KCCI contacted Nathan. Eric wanted to do a story on them. A native Iowan, Eric did special interest stories on people in Central Iowa. He produced a two-minute "Battling back against the odds," segment that aired several times on October 25, 2012. Included in the segment was the GiveForward website. This had an immediate impact on "Help Laura Win." Three months after KCCI aired the segment the fund reached $20,000. Eric was sensitive to Laura and Nathan's circumstances. He produced the story in a professional and respectful manner. Eric had earned the trust of Nathan.

Dr. Angela Franklin became the president and CEO of Des Moines University (DMU) shortly before Laura experienced the "stroke" event in March 2011. Dr. Franklin's Executive Leadership Team (ELT) included senior management leaders at DMU. The college deans were members of the ELT. Dr. Franklin started a tradition of identifying an opportunity to provide financial assistance to an individual or family as part of the giving spirit over the winter holiday season. In November 2012, being aware of Laura's condition, she wanted to know if I was comfortable with Laura and Nathan being selected as the recipients of the ELT holiday gift. She indicated the other members of the ELT were fully supportive. I expressed my appreciation and agreed as long as I could participate. Dr. Franklin announced the gift at her annual holiday gathering for ELT members and friends. The gift did not come as a surprise—the amount did.

Laura and Nathan attended an ELT meeting after receiving the gift to thank the group for their generosity. It was an emotional moment for everyone. A year later, Nathan and Caralyn received the ELT gift. This came as a surprise to me. It was an emotional moment for Donna and me. We were grateful for the support from Dr. Franklin and my professional colleagues.

After Laura passed, as we were going through some of Laura belongings, we came across a stack of envelopes. Inside were a variety of cards offering well wishes and encouragement for Laura. The cards were signed by the same person.

We came to learn in the final months of Laura's life, Joe's father-in-law, Dennis, would send a card with a financial gift on a weekly basis telling her to treat herself to something. Neither Laura nor Dennis ever said a word.

The CrossFit community is a close-knit group. You have

the chance to meet people from diverse backgrounds having one thing in common: fitness. CrossFitters are notorious for pushing and cheering each other on to finish the workout of the day (WOD), whether you have fastest time, slowest time, lift the most, or the least.

The Noyce family, owners of CrossFit 515, wanted to do something for Nathan. In the spirit of how the CrossFit community honors people, and knowing how hard Laura worked to survive, a memorial WOD called Another Kind of Strong was held on August 24, 2014. Hundreds of athletes representing CrossFit gyms from across Iowa descended on CrossFit 515 in Grimes.

Many participants knew Laura or Nathan, many did not. I met Eric, a former teammate of Nathan's in Little League. They were on opposing sides of the field in several high school sports.

Eric, living in Iowa City, a couple of hours from Des Moines, heard about the event and felt he needed to come and show his support. I do not believe Eric and Nathan had seen each other in over ten years.

The honor WOD generated over $10,000 to assist Nathan cover the costs of Laura's medical expenses. Every time I drive by CrossFit 515, I am reminded of the compassion and generosity we experienced that day.

The compassion provided to Laura and Nathan extended well beyond fundraising. They received hundreds of cards and letters during Laura's illness and continued to pour in after her death. Nathan did not expect one letter dated August 7, 2013. It read:

> *Dear Nate:*
>
> *Thank you so much for speaking with me on July 23, 2013, the day Laura passed away.*
>
> *It has taken me some time to collect my thoughts about Laura and you before being able to write this letter.*
>
> *I know that you know better than anyone else how an amazingly strong woman Laura was. I do not recollect a single moment when she would complain about her diagnosis and disabilities. Even when I broke bad news to Laura and to you, even though tears were shed, she would pick herself up and then look to the future for further therapies with hope. Then, when we ran out of therapies to offer, Laura faced that situation with unparalleled courage.*
>
> *I will forever remember Laura's contagious smile, and her inner strength. I will remember the many videos that you would send me of her working out at the gym despite having a brain tumor diagnosis. I remember especially well how she was still walking in a recent video that you sent even with the*

difficulties that she had in terms of controlling her arm and leg.

Moreover, I will remember how you took such loving care of her. You looked after every one of her needs. You would search the world for various treatment options and try everything in your power to get her the best treatment possible. Then, when no further treatment could be done you comforted her.

I know that Laura's spirit will live on in all your hearts and her daughter.

It has simply been my privilege to get to know Laura and you as well as your families.

You and Laura embody the definition of courage and inspire me and my colleagues to do our utmost to find better treatments for patients afflicted with this horrible disease. With my deepest sympathies and condolences,

Joon H. Uhm, M.D.

With permission from Nathan, I have used parts of this letter at Des Moines University's annual White Coat Ceremonies to demonstrate the virtue of medical professionalism. On many occasions, I have been approached by students and by parents of students who attended the event to extend their appreciation for sharing Nathan's letter.

Shortly after Caralyn's birth, Nathan received several

packages, the contents of which needed to be immediately stored in a freezer. A friend of Laura's from college and now a physician specializing in obstetrics had recently given birth to her own baby. She continued to pump with the purpose of Caralyn, at least for as long as the supply lasted. She wanted Caralyn to receive the health benefits of breast milk. Another friend of Nathan's did the same. The supply lasted six months. The date the milk was produced was neatly inscribed on each plastic bag.

Early on, Donna, Nathan, and I took turns with Caralyn's late feeding. Even a novice could follow the procedure for thawing and warming the milk. I did encounter a misadventure one evening. Whether there was a defect in the bag or a problem with the technician's process remains an unsolved mystery. As I was preparing Caralyn's feeding, a warm bag of milk without warning burst, the contents making a direct hit to my face. It was impossible to avoid sampling the liquid gold.

As an infant, Caralyn did not have colds, ear infections, or other common pediatric illnesses. We credit the milk Caralyn received for getting her off to a healthy start. She was blessed to have Laura and Nathan's friends think about her while caring for their own children.

On October 18, 2013, Nathan's close friend, member of his wedding party, and mixed martial arts fighter Paul appeared on Spike TV. On his sponsor banner and located on the back of Paul's waist band was the message, "Show Love for Laura." It was Paul's way of honoring Laura and supporting his friend. Paul won his match. He made it a point to highlight "Show Love for Laura" when the ring announcer called out his name as the winner. Nathan appreciated the gesture seen by thousands of people.

Chris, a friend of Kara, Aaron, and Nathan, embarked on an eight-day journey to climb Mt. Kilimanjaro as part of the Survivors Summit Program in association with the LIVESTRONG Foundation. The program covers the cost of cancer survivors capable of making the climb to Uhuru peak, the summit of Mount Kilimanjaro. The name comes from the Swahili word for freedom. Standing at a height of 19,341 feet above sea level, Uhuru Peak holds the title of the highest point in the whole of Africa and second in the world. On February 19, 2014, Chris reached Uhuru peak. The team of climbers included Laura's name adorned on the summit flag. As Chris looked to the horizon, he felt that much closer to Kara and Aaron's friend, and Nathan's wife.

A number of months after Laura died, the editor of the Des Moines University Magazine, a biannual update for news and events at DMU, asked me to author an article about our experience. It was titled, *"What to say? What to do?"* Des Moines University granted me permissioin to reprint the article published on May 26, 2014.

> *One of the things I have always struggled with as a person and a health care provider is how to approach a friend, a colleague, a patient who is having personal challenges. How do you let them know you are thinking of them without running the risk of being viewed as overly intrusive or just plain nosey? All of us have experienced difficult times, and we know many friends and colleagues who have as well. Whether it be illness or loss of a friend or a loved one, there is an internal mechanism that causes us to want to help. The problem is what to say or what to do?*
>
> *Our family story—the loss of our beautiful daughter-in-law Laura to brain cancer, and circumstances of the birth of our granddaughter Caralyn—have been well chronicled. Laura and Nathan were a perfect couple. They battled her disease as a team and lived as normal a life as possible under exceedingly difficult circumstances: three brain surgeries, radiation, and countless rounds of chemotherapy over a 27-month period. Laura lost her battle on July 23, 2013.*
>
> *My wife, Donna, Nathan, and I are private people. We tend to not openly discuss personal issues, the exception being the few individuals who we feel should have some knowledge of the situation.*

Laura and Nathan were a popular couple; they knew a lot of people. Her battle against cancer was covered in various media as a featured news item to help others continue to fight the good fight through exercise and wellness. Word travels quickly.

Throughout Laura's illness and following her death, we have been overwhelmed by the compassion, love, and support shown to us by so many people in so many ways—family, friends, neighbors, colleagues, Laura's physicians, and people we have never met. We are so blessed to be surrounded by so many caring people.

From this experience, we have learned much in terms of how we should interact with people who are experiencing a difficult time. And this is what we learned:

1. *It does not matter whether people are private or not.*

2. *Let someone know you are thinking of them or you are hoping for the best rather than asking how everything going or how is the person doing. That can be an uncomfortable question to answer. Just let the person offer if he or she wants.*

3. *Be a good listener.*

4. *If you are not comfortable with a face-to-face*

> *approach, just send a simple "thinking of you" note or card.*
>
> 5. *Don't ask "What can I do?" Just do something you feel would be helpful.*
> 6. *Don't compare your own experience with the person's circumstance.*
>
> *Doing one or more of these simple things helps far beyond what you can imagine. And lastly, avoiding the situation is a lost opportunity for you to bring comfort to someone and experience a feeling of goodness.*
>
> *So, what appears to be a complex question and places us in an uncomfortable position really turns out to have a simple answer, with thoughtful meaning. Make it a point to tell someone or send a note that you are thinking of them. The effect is profound.*

Compassion and generosity are terms that are loosely thrown around. You realize the power of these virtues when you are on both the receiving end and when you are the donor.

Keeping a Promise: Barbells and the Purple Rose

Laura and Nathan talked a lot about owning their own gym. They both had a passion for fitness and desire to help people with their health. Laura had been involved in fitness since graduating from college and Nathan since he had retired from professional baseball. Having firsthand knowledge of the business, they felt they had the experience and motivation to run a successful gym.

As members of CrossFit 515, a CrossFit affiliate in Grimes, they enjoyed the community environment of the gym and the variety of movements integrated into the daily WOD. One day might be focused on Olympic lifts and rowing, the next day gymnastic movements and rope climbs. CrossFit 515 was a place where people of all ages and backgrounds gathered and suffered in unison through the WOD. Albeit difficult, it was a respite from the daily challenges of life, at least for an hour. It provided the template for what Laura and Nathan had envisioned for themselves. Even as Laura's health began to decline, they continued to talk about how they looked forward to achieving this goal.

After Laura died, the grieving process and preparing for the arrival of Caralyn occupied much of Nathan's time and thoughts. He had to deal with the emotional disparity of these two significant life-changing events.

Nathan took some time off after Laura's funeral. When he finally returned to work, it wasn't the same. It was difficult for him knowing Laura was no longer there. Fellow employees and clients had good intentions but it became a challenge to answer the same questions on a continuous basis. It didn't feel right.

In early October, Nathan left his job to just do personal training in a garage gym he had created at his home. This would give him the chance to be close to Caralyn when she arrived. He had made a promise to start a gym. Nathan would know when the timing was right.

We had agreed it would be best for Donna and I to move in with Nathan after Caralyn was born. Moving from a 2,700 square foot home with two adults and a small dog to a 1,600 square foot home with three adults, a newborn, a dog, and two cats would be an adjustment. We were all committed to making it work.

Two months after we moved in, everyone seemed to be settling into a new routine. At that time, Nathan made the decision it was time to open his own gym. He began the search for a location.

Based on the experience at CrossFit 515, Nathan was going the CrossFit route. It wasn't long before he found an available space in a building on Merle Hay Road near the Merle Hay Mall, a high-traffic shopping area that bordered on the cities of Urbandale and Des Moines. The building currently housed a Carlos O'Kelly's restaurant, a bar, and a space, formerly a salon, that had been vacant for almost ten years.

In the dead of an Iowa winter, with heat siphoned from the adjacent bar, Nathan and a couple of friends he recruited did the demo work, usually in the evenings. Between water pipes freezing and bursting, requiring the local fire department to shut off the water, to removing moldy drywall, the final result was an open space for him to build their gym. During this time,

Donna would be the primary caregiver to Caralyn while Nathan and I filled in the gaps and worked our daily jobs.

Nathan secured a loan and planned every detail of the

gym. He acted as his own contractor. Through connections he made and relationships he had established over the years, Nathan hired individuals to complete various parts of the project. There were setbacks and frustrations but his commitment to the project never wavered. His target date to open the gym would be March 7, 2014, Laura's birthday.

The gym would be licensed under the name CrossFit Merle Hay. He did this for two reasons. The Merle Hay address assigned a location to the gym and honored Merle Hay, a twenty-one year old a farm boy from Glidden, Iowa, believed to be one of three and possibly the first American soldier killed in World War I on November 3, 1917, in the fields of Artois, France. This became the naming protocol Nathan followed for two other gyms he would open in the future: to honor people.

To market the gym, Nathan used various forms of social media, showing the progress being made in building out the gym. Before long he had enlisted many volunteers to assist with painting, setting the floor, organizing the equipment, stocking CrossFit Merle Hay merchandise, and prepping for the grand opening. The gym had already achieved that spirit of community.

Prior to opening day, I had the chance to visit the gym with Nathan. When you walk into CrossFit Merle Hay your eyes are drawn to a couple of things. First are the

KEEPING A PROMISE: BARBELLS AND THE PURPLE ROSE

gray walls with the white and purple wood trim. Next is the large logo consisting of barbells forming a cross with a purple rose in the center. The purple rose would be present on nearly every piece of merchandise sold at the gym.

The meaning behind the colors and symbols are simple but intentional. The gray represents brain cancer, purple was Laura's favorite color, the crossed bar bells signify faith, and then there is the rose. The first flower Nathan gave to Laura was a white rose. It signifies love. Laura loved roses; it marked the good times and challenging times. They were present at Laura's wedding and her funeral. The final item is a glass case with a pair of worn purple Reebok CrossFit Nano shoes. They were Laura's—a small reminder of her continued presence at the gym.

When people ask about the symbolism, they are given a brief summary of Laura's fight to live and the story of Caralyn. When you are in the middle of a WOD and you feel like quitting, the symbols remind people of what Laura went through and to help them push through the workout. The logo would become well known in the Midwest CrossFit community.

CrossFit Merle Hay opened as planned with a large turnout on March 7, 2014. Laura would have been thirty-one years old—a promise kept.

Raising Caralyn

Caralyn's room had the most recent technology to monitor her every movement and sound. Donna was on call for night one. Everything was going well when the monitor captured Caralyn crying. It had been thirty years since we had heard that sound. Donna woke up and asked me, "What's that?" I scanned the room and heard the sounds on the monitor. There were three silhouettes at the end of the bed. I responded to Donna by saying, "That's Lou, Oliver, and Brewer (our dog), and I hear Caralyn crying. Welcome to our new life."

There's nothing overly exciting about the day-to-day life of taking care of an infant. Donna found a pediatrician for Caralyn. Nathan would always accompany Donna and Caralyn for appointments. The three of us settled into a routine fairly quickly. Nathan and I would work during the week while Donna was the primary caregiver to Caralyn during the day. We took turns tending to Caralyn during the evening in accordance with our on-call schedule. It took a few lessons but Nathan and I eventually became proficient at processing the donated frozen bags of breast milk for on-time feedings and changing a diaper. Caralyn's nursery was off limits for Lou and Oliver. We granted Brewer an occasional supervised visit. As Caralyn became familiar with the people around her, Donna became Nonna, I became Pop-pop and Nathan, Daddy. Lenore and Doug had more traditional grandparent names, Grandma and Gramps.

Pictures of Laura, Laura and Nathan, and Kara in a group photo of Laura's close friends from college were hung in Caralyn's bedroom and throughout Nathan's home. It was important that Caralyn see images of her mother as much as possible.

The rocking chair Laura and Nathan gave to Donna on Mother's Day stayed in Caralyn's room. There's nothing like the feeling of rocking your granddaughter in the middle of the night and seeing her eyes gently close.

Leaving Aspen and doing private personal training in his garage gym gave Nathan more time to be with Caralyn. It also provided the opportunity to achieve their goal of owning a gym and keeping his promise. In addition to the resident people and animals, we had a steady stream of Nathan's clients training in the garage.

LIFE AFTER DEATH: THE LAURA AND CARALYN YOHO STORY

On May 31, 2014, six months after Caralyn was born, we traveled to Wilton for a special day. Caralyn would be baptized in the church where her parents were married and Laura's funeral service had been held.

In the tradition of Donna's family, Caralyn would be the ninth baby girl baptized in the same christening gown. Kara was Caralyn's Godmother and Joe her Godfather. Father Bob performed the baptismal ceremony. He acknowledged the tragedy and triumphs our families had experienced over the past several years. He singled out Nathan for commitment to Laura and now to Caralyn. He asked everyone to provide guidance to Caralyn, noting the importance of faith in her life. Even this experience was new for Father Bob.

Donna and I lived with Nathan and Caralyn for slightly over three years. During that time, CrossFit Merle Hay steadily grew with a dedicated membership and Caralyn's schedule became fairly consistent. The time had come for Nathan to have his own space. As difficult as it was to leave Caralyn on a full-time basis, Donna and I needed to return to our own home. We pulled up stakes after the 2016–2017 winter holidays. Nathan continually let us know of his gratitude for our support throughout our stay.

During the time we lived in Grimes, I would check on our home several times a week with an occasional stayover. Our neighbors helped keep watch. As Caralyn grew, Donna and I would gradually increase the number of overnight stays at our house. It was part of the process to prepare us for reentry on a full-time basis. Even after the move, Donna would still take care of Caralyn during the day. She would stay with us Tuesday nights and an occasional weekend night. When we moved back permanently, time seemed to have stood still. Nothing had changed, yet everything had changed.

For three years, we were blessed to watch Caralyn grow, hit developmental milestones, celebrate birthdays and holidays, and observe Nathan do everything in his power to give her as normal life as possible while continuing to honor Laura's life.

We made sure Laura was a constant in her life. In the family room were two beautiful portraits of their wedding day. When Caralyn visited her grandparents in Wilton, she would see pictures of Laura with her family. We purposely read books to her about heaven and angels.

After Caralyn turned two, on Laura's next birthday, we celebrated with a cake and candles. Caralyn led us in song and blew out the candles. We let Caralyn release purple balloons into the sky. She would watch until they disappeared from view. She was sending them to her mommy in heaven. When she became a little older, she would include a message on the balloons. This is repeated every year. At about the same time in her life, we started taking her to the Oakdale Cemetery in Wilton to visit Laura's resting place. She would leave a bouquet that always included purple flowers or a stuffed animals she would pick out especially for her mommy.

Toward the end of our stay with Nathan, Caralyn began to make comments about Laura. She would say how pretty she was and tell us how much she wished she could hug her. There were a few times she felt sad because her mommy could not hold her. Another time she told us her mommy visited her at night when she is sleeping. We could not help but agree. I once took Caralyn outside to see Laura's star. After that, she loved to sing "Twinkle, Twinkle Little Star."

In the fall of 2017, Caralyn would attend preschool. She had been around adults most of her life who knew her story. This would be the first experience with other children for an extended length of time. Her circumstances were different. We did not know to what extent this would affect her, as children will be children with limited filters. To date, she hasn't informed us of anything being said that was upsetting to her. Hopefully, that trend will continue. We understand at some point Caralyn will need to respond to questions or comments.

Her teachers are consistent in their evaluations of her. They love her; it's easy to do. Her favorite subjects are recess followed by math and spelling. With increased frequency we see her put her iPad down and pick of a book and read. She does need to improve on the neatness of her writing skills—something she inherited from her father and a long line of Yohos.

Although Caralyn enjoys being with other children, you can tell she prefers one-on-one relationships rather than being in a large group. When she attended activities that involved a group of children with their mothers present, Caralyn would periodically retreat to Donna or her father. Donna recalls attending one of Caralyn's school friend's birthday parties where most of the mothers of the children were in attendance. She told Donna, "I know you're not my mommy but it is OK if I call you mommy?" The answer was yes. There is a sensitivity about her.

Caralyn has an impressive imagination. Her storytelling ability is unmatched. She tends to be the featured character in her stories that are frequently based her favorite cartoon or YouTube personality of the day. It could range from My Little Ponies, to Shimmer and Shine, her collection of fidgets, creating a story with Legos, or her stuffed animals. She has been to Disney World, visited the Magic Kingdom, and had her picture taken with Mickey. Her favorite, Minnie, was unavailable. In the spirit of technology, she likes to FaceTime her best friend, and one cousin in particular. The conversations are fascinating.

From an early age, much like her father, Caralyn enjoys art and making things. She paints everything, including rocks, her Play-Doh figures, self-portraits, and any other items she might discover while playing outside. She once painted a large piece of wood that splintered from a tree in our front yard after it was damaged by a storm. She painted it in the form of a rainbow.

Her colors are always the light and bright. Caralyn is always doing something with her hands. Making small figures out Play-Doh, giving them names, and creating communities is a favorite activity she likes to do based on the number of these little creatures found throughout our home.

Caralyn has a unique skill in that after hearing a song a few times, she quickly picks up on the lyrics and will sing the song in its entirety. We are mindful as to what she listens to. Her ability to recite things in short time also occurs with common statements of commitment, such as the Pledge of Allegiance, the Lord's Prayer, The Hail Mary Prayer, and other such statements or oaths.

In late September, nearly every year, the monarch butterflies migrating from Canada to Mexico make a stop in the lot next to our home. It's an amazing scene. Hundreds of butterflies for days come and go. Caralyn looks forward to seeing the monarchs every year. She catches a few in her net but always releases them. The butterfly is one of her favorite things.

As one might expect, Caralyn is very close to her father. They play, they laugh, and they tease each other. Every day they tell each other how much they love each other. After we moved back to West Des Moines, Nathan made it a point to take Fridays off to be with Caralyn. Swimming and playgrounds are their most popular playdates. Or it might be that they just spend time together drawing or painting.

When her focus was dinosaurs, he took her to a dinosaur exhibit at the Iowa Events Center. When her favorite pop star JoJo Siwa came to Des Moines for a concert, Nathan bought tickets for her sixth birthday that included a backstage pass. She talked about meeting JoJo for weeks.

With Caralyn's first softball season at age seven, most of the fathers were giving their daughters constant instructions while Nathan, who clearly had more experience than all the fathers, would occasionally give her a piece of advice. Most important to him was that she have fun interacting with her teammates and learn the fundamentals of the game. Regardless of the outcome, to build her confidence, she is complemented on her performance. When Nathan drops her off or we pick her up they always part by saying, "I love you," followed by two quick pecks on the lips in the same way he would kiss Laura.

Caralyn is athletic but is not all that interested in sports other than swimming, which she probably doesn't realize can be a sport. When it comes to clothing, she is a fashionista in what she wears—Donna is somewhat responsible for that—and in what she selects or designs for her Barbie dolls. Bows are an essential accessory.

She is polite and well mannered. "Please" and "Thank you" are constants in her vocabulary. Her mannerisms depend on what type of mood she is in and how you catch her at a particular moment. There are times you believe you are looking at a little Laura and other times a little Nathan. The one thing she gets from both of her parents is a positive outlook. Negativity around her is not permitted. She is the perfect blend of Laura, Nathan, and herself.

As far as her relationship with Laura's family. The Brammeiers were in a difficult position. Losing Laura at such a young age followed by the birth of her daughter spans the spectrum of emotions. Grieving takes time. After the initial joy of Caralyn's birth, it was a challenge for Lenore and Doug to balance the sense of loss with this new person who represented her. It's also difficult to develop a relationship with an infant you don't see on a frequent basis.

The relationship between the Brammeiers evolved as Caralyn grew and developed over the years. As the grieving for Laura lessens—it never goes away—their attention is directed more toward Caralyn. The interactions have increased in number and quality. Caralyn is excited when she gets to stay with Grandma and Gramps. A bonus is when Joe and Katy's children visit at the same time.

Caralyn maintains a terrific relationship with Kara and her family. They don't see each other in person all that frequently, but do stay in contact. Kara has attended every one of Caralyn's birthday celebrations. To Caralyn she is Aunt Kara. But she is also old enough to know Aunt Kara carried her. There is a special bond.

We talk to Caralyn about Laura when the moment appears right or she asks about her. This has increased as she has gotten older. She likes when we tell her something about herself that reminds us of Laura: her looks, her movements, her positive attitude. She has seen videos of Laura and knows they are available to her. It's difficult for her to process her life at such a young age. As she grows her curiosity will grow. Nathan is prepared to tell and show her how special her mommy was and how hard she tried to be here with her.

Caralyn is many things. Her life story is complex. To us she is simply a gift from God with help from many people and a little science mixed in. We look forward to the day when she is able to understand her circumstances and we can ask her a simple question, "What do you think?"

Paying It Forward

Nathan has always been a caring individual. If asked to help someone, he would. The experiences he had throughout Laura's ordeal with brain cancer only fortified this value. His approach in the past was more reactive in nature. After Laura died, his desire to help others became more deliberate.

The one thing he discovered in educating himself on brain tumors was how little funding came from the public sector, governmental agencies, and charity organizations for brain cancer. Breast cancer by far receives the most funding, followed by leukemia, childhood cancers, and lymphoma. These cancers all receive a greater share of funding relative to their proportion of total new cancer cases, mortality, and years of life lost. In contrast, brain cancer is one of the most underfunded cancers relative to those same metrics.

Nathan's first order of business would be to help raise funds for brain cancer. In the spring of 2014, he participated in two local runs dedicated to brain cancer. His goal was to raise $1,500 for each race. The enticement to meet his goal was to shave off a robust beard he had been growing since Laura's death. He raised $4,134. From this experience, he realized going with one organization committed to funding brain cancer research and providing assistance locally to individuals diagnosed with cancer would be a better strategy. After researching a number of organizations, the Head for the Cure Foundation aligned well with his priorities. The mission of Head for the Cure was:

> *To raise awareness and funding to inspire hope for the community of brain cancer patients, their families, friends, caregivers, and other supporters, while celebrating their courage, spirit, and energy.*

Head for the Cure organizes 5K runs/walks and other events in a number of cities across the United States dedicated to raising funds in support of brain cancer research. That support includes the Brain Tumor Trials Collaborative and giving back to the local community. Having an impact locally was important to Nathan.

He reached out to the headquarters of the national

organization in Kansas City to learn more about the Head for the Cure Foundation. At the same time, I was serving on an advisory board at a cancer center affiliated with one of the major healthcare systems in Des Moines. Between the two organization, Nathan, and myself, we reached an agreement. If the cancer center would serve as a sponsor to the 5K run, their foundation would be the local beneficiary.

Over the next three years, Nathan's team, Laura's Fight to Win, was the top fundraising team for the Des Moines Head for the Cure 5K run. The local cancer center received a gift in the $2,500–$5,000 range each year. During that time, Nathan raised close to $30,000. He continues to raise awareness and funds for brain cancer research.

One of Nathan's business partners and CrossFit Merle Hay coaches, Caileen, approached Nathan about a new fundraising competition, Barbells for Boobs. The competition involved CrossFit gyms across Iowa raising money for breast cancer. Nearly every member of CrossFit Merle Hay had been touched by breast cancer. Nathan agreed. For two consecutive years, Barbells for Boobs recognized CrossFit Merle Hay as the top fundraising gym. In two years, they raised over $10,000. CrossFit Merle Hay continues to sponsor events in support of breast cancer.

Nathan recognized the philanthropic role the gym

could have in benefiting other organizations, including the Food Bank of Iowa, the ValorFit Foundation (an organization dedicated to assisting military veterans regain their health and confidence by purchasing memberships to fitness facilities and gyms), and to see that children at Orchard Place, an organization providing mental health treatment to children, receive a gift they requested for Christmas.

Nathan's generosity extends beyond organizations. He agreed to meet with Daniel, a writer for the Des Moines Register assigned to author a story about Laura and Nathan. Nathan has a good sense about people. After speaking to Daniel, he felt Daniel was someone he could trust to share his story. The article, "A Love Story," in Daniel's words, "Was an unconventional love story involving a beautiful woman and a handsome man who married. They wanted to have a baby, but couldn't. So, the woman's best friend offered to carry the baby for them. This is also a tragedy. It involves brain tumors, cancer, and the struggle to survive against a relentless disease. Through it all, though, this remains a love story." It was published in the Des Moines Register on July 27, 2013, the day of Laura's funeral.

Daniel published a follow-up article on December 20, 2013, titled, "A Special Delivery." In the article, Daniel penned a letter to Caralyn. The letter began with:

Dear Caralyn,

You are barely a month old now, too young to read this letter. But one day soon, someone will show you this, and maybe it will help you understand the wonderful confluence of love and hope that you brought into this world on November 26, 2013.

The closing section of the letter read:

Caralyn, your mom died before you drew your first breath. That's not fair. But you will know her. Your dad has videos, your grandparents have pictures and stories. And your surrogate mom, Kara, she's got stories, too. Nobody will ever take the place of the mom you didn't get the chance to meet. But these kind, selfless people are going to make sure you have everything your mom wanted you to have. And what she wanted you to have more than anything in this world is love and hope. The next time you're at a family gathering, look around at the faces of all these people who helped you get here. That's when you will see and feel your mom the most.

Years later Daniel would say the letter to Caralyn remains the best thing he has written in a career spanning twenty-three years.

The relationship between Daniel and Nathan would

continue. In late December 2014, Daniel injured his back. The injury became chronic. When asked if he needed a wheelchair while doing a story at a hospital, Daniel recognized it was time for a change. He began a weekly update about his recovery in a Des Moines Register Blog titled "Making Weight."

Nathan began to follow Daniel's progress. He texted Daniel to invite him to workout at CrossFit Merle Hay under his supervision. Daniel reluctantly agreed. Over the next year, Nathan was a frequent figure in Daniel's blog. They shared stories and talked about the challenges each of them faced. Their relationship became personal. I believe Nathan wanted Daniel's overall health to improve as much as Daniel did. Over the course of 2016 there was progress and there were setbacks. In the article, "Giving Thanks for Help with Health," published in the Des Moines Register on November 23, 2016, Daniel provided a summary of his journey to improve his health. Daniel had lost over 100 pounds and noted improvement in his strength and mental well-being. Daniel offered a list of reasons to thank Nathan. The article concluded with:

> *Thank you for every challenge, every encouragement, every kindness. Most of all, Nate, thank you for being my friend. I often say this to you. You accept the gratitude, but remind me our friendship is not a favor. Nonetheless, I am grateful beyond my*

capabilities to express the sentiment. We may have met on one of the worst days of your life, but our continued work together ensures my days continue to get better. So, thank you, Nate Yoho. Your friendship honors me.

Nathan needed to make a decision. As years passed, he came to the realization that it was unlikely he would have another child from the few remaining cryopreserved embryos still housed in the office of the fertility practice. Reaching that conclusion, he considered three options. The embryos could be donated for scientific purposes, destroyed, or donated to a couple experiencing fertility issues.

There are complex moral, ethical, and religious factors that come into play when making such a weighty decision. Nathan and Laura were Catholic. Catholic doctrine does not support IVF. Nathan and Laura were able to rationalize the use of IVF under the circumstances with the support of their families. After all, in the words of Pope Francis, "Who am I to judge," when commenting on another controversial issue in the Catholic Church. Those words could easily apply to Laura and Nathan's situation. A phrase that was later quoted by Father Bob. Catholic doctrine also rejects the destruction of an embryo.

There were other factors in play, not the least of which was what Laura had to endure with the ovarian stimulation procedure and subsequent pain she had experienced with OHSS. The idea of Caralyn at some point having a genetic sibling was also appealing. In the end, it wasn't a difficult decision. Although the idea may not have been fully endorsed by all family members, there were no strong objections.

After Nathan shared his decision with family members, with his approval, I researched several embryo adoption agencies and provided him with my findings. With his continued permission, I reached out to Maria, president and cofounder of Embryo Adoption Services of Cedar Park, located in Washington State. Maria reviewed the process to donate the remaining embryos and the recipient selection process.

The initial step required submitting an application that included basic demographic information and physical characteristics of the donors, the personal medical history of the donors, and the family health history to include the donors' parents, siblings, grandparents, aunts, uncles, and first cousins. The application requested information on the fertility clinic where the embryos were housed and a signed release of medical information form granting permission for the fertility clinic to release Laura's medical record. A final form identified the preferred relationship by the donor.

Donna and I, and Laura's parents agreed to move forward with the process by providing the information requested. You could sense the difficulty Lenore and Doug would have completing the background information on Laura.

Any recipient under consideration undergoes a similar comprehensive review as well, including a home study, involving background checks and an in-person home visit by a social worker from the adoption agency.

In time, Nathan received a letter from Maria indicating the agency had identified a couple deemed to be a good match. Maria shared a letter from the couple expressing their gratitude for being considered to receive the embryos. After reviewing the information provided to him, Nathan granted his approval for the couple.

Nathan and Laura had done for this couple what Kara and Aaron had done for them. Hopefully, one day Caralyn will get the chance to meet a genetic sibling.

Nathan paid it forward and then some.

Laura and Nathan

Donna and I knew Laura for almost four and a half years. Half of that time, Laura was undergoing treatment for her illness. It sounds cliché, but from the moment we met her, Donna and I knew Nathan had found the right person.

Laura was as beautiful as Nathan is handsome. There is no other way to state it. They were both college educated and loved what they were doing. When we met her, they were in their mid-twenties, full of energy, with their entire lives ahead of them.

They had so much in common yet, enough differences to keep each other balanced. They both loved fitness but their approaches were different—Nathan more measured and goal oriented, Laura more of a risk-taker, following the idea-of-the-day philosophy. Nathan preferred saving money. Laura liked to spend.

They came from different backgrounds but were respectful of the differences. Both valued family, immediate, and extended. Holidays were important and they found a way to divide time between the Brammeier and Yoho families. If you did something to help them, even in the slightest, you received a thank-you card, a text, or a phone call.

When they were together, they stayed close to each other. Teasing and joking were in play but neither ever said anything that would diminish or embarrass the other. They both had a terrific sense of humor—Laura had no choice being raised with Joe. They loved to laugh.

Laura appeared to be the aggressor when it came to public displays of affection (PDA). From our experience that was not in Nathan's romance tool bag. Being close to each other was the extent of Nathan's PDA. That changed after Laura's diagnosis and she underwent more surgeries and supplemental treatments. Not knowing if the person you love is going to survive a surgery or respond to a treatment causes behaviors to change. Hugs were much more common and two quick kisses on the lips signaled their love for one another and that everything would be fine.

It did not matter if they were with a group or just the two of them, they just enjoyed being around each other and people enjoyed being around them. Through Nathan's friends and connections—and he had many—opportunities came around. They went to Anaheim, California, to cheer on Paul in a UFC match. They ended up at the after-fight party chumming with celebrities and top UFC fighters. They had no trouble fitting in.

They liked to travel and took every advantage as Laura's health permitted, be it the gulf side beaches of Florida, the scenic West Coast, or the casinos and bright lights of Las Vegas.

When you met them, you could not tell they were dealing with a serious medical condition—at least until Laura's disabilities became noticeable. They did not bring it up. If someone asked, their response was always positive. They did what they could until it was no longer possible.

When Laura and Kara talked about Kara carrying her baby, they did not discuss the possibility of Laura not being at the birth. I am sure it crossed their minds. Laura's belief was, "Whatever happens, happens. A baby is a joy to all no matter what." That was how she viewed her circumstances.

Given the opportunity to help others, both did not hesitate to offer assistance. When Nathan was playing professional minor league baseball for the West Virginia Power, he was penned in the starting lineup card for the final game of a long season. They were playing the Hickory Crawdads (North Carolina). It had been a difficult season for Nathan. With the hand injury and having three other younger and incredibly talented outfielders on the team, his future with the Brewers did not appear very promising. A brief unexpected thunderstorm prior to the first pitch washed out the game. Nathan knew this was most likely his last game in the Brewer organization. As he left the dugout, he saw a young boy upset over the game being cancelled. Knowing his own situation and disappointment, Nathan approached the boy and gave him his bat and his batting gloves. To the boy it was better than the game. I learned about this story from Frank, who attended the game, saw the exchange, and spoke to the boy's father. Nathan's actions were a sign of things to come.

After graduating from St. Ambrose University, Laura dedicated her time, energy, and talents to help family members, friends, and groups she would volunteer with to speak with about importance of nutrition and living a healthy lifestyle. Nothing satisfied Laura more than to see a person take control of their life. She made herself available to anyone who asked for her assistance. We continue to be confounded by what happened to an individual who did everything to model a healthy lifestyle. If there was one message Laura would want people to hear, it would be to take care of themselves through nutrition and fitness.

A year after Laura's diagnosis, a young woman in a nearby community was diagnosed with the same condition. Laura reached out to her, letting her know she was not alone in this battle and for her feel free to contact Laura anytime if she needed someone to talk to or lean on. She died shortly after we lost Laura. Later, the mother of the young woman spoke to Laura's parents. She expressed her sympathies on their loss and her gratitude for the comfort Laura provided to her daughter.

Following the wedding, Donna and I received a letter from Debbie. She had trained with Laura and Nathan. Her son played on the same high school hockey team as Nathan. As parents it's easy to be biased about your own children. Debbie wanted us to know her thoughts on Nathan, commenting on his energy and caring style. He frequently mentioned both of us to Debbie and what we had done for him growing up. She let Donna know how much Laura appreciated what she had done for her and so very much enjoyed the time they spent together.

Courage, compassion, loyalty, determination, and love are just a few of the core values we witnessed from Laura and Nathan over the last twenty-seven months of Laura's life. They continue today as part of Nathan's daily life. He can be a little rough around the edges and we have different perspectives of what is best, but what you get from Nathan is real and genuine.

After Laura's death, Nathan's activities were more purposeful with a specific reason for his involvement. Aside from the cancer initiatives and other worthy causes he helped champion, Nathan opened a second gym and became a partner at an existing third gym. The gym he opened was named CrossFit Valley Junction in West Des Moines. Valley Junction became a prominent railroad town in the late 1800s. Prior to that, Valley Junction was a stop along the way as part of the Underground Railroad. The Valley Junction name was selected to honor the men and women who work in the railroad industry. The logo is a locomotive.

Nathan convinced his new female partner at the existing gym to change the name of the gym located in a growing area of downtown Des Moines. They selected Black Collar CrossFit to recognize individuals working in the mining and oil industries, with special attention to female workers. The logo is a female miner with helmet and pickaxe.

Both logos include the Purple Rose. He continues to look for opportunities to help others and highlight groups of individuals who often go unrecognized or under appreciated.

Toward the end of Laura's life, she gave Nathan a card. The card read:

> Nathan,
>
> I love you. I love the fact that I'm a better person with. You are my best friend. You make my day better by just the thought of you. You make me push myself to do things I would never do without you. You are the best husband ever and I am so fortunate to have you. Even though some people might think I'm unlucky and they might feel sorry for me, I feel I am the luckiest girl ever because I get to go home with you every night. Thank you for everything you do for us. I love you.
>
> Laura

The card and the challenges Laura faced to put her thoughts into writing that note, more than anything else, captures the relationship between Laura and Nathan. Laura will always be the love of his life, just as Nathan was the love of Laura's life. With Caralyn, Nathan must now share that designation.

Life Goes On

We have all heard the expression, "Life goes on." Unfortunately, it has become more of a platitude. What can't be discounted is understanding the reason that brought that phrase into play. It is all relative and must be put into perspective. We use it to console a teenager after losing an important game, or when someone we have worked with for a long time retires and is replaced. But what does it mean when the event is a serious illness or the loss of a loved one?

Important components of "life goes on" are the lessons learned and actions taken to adapt to the changes caused by the event, especially when the outcome is life-changing. The story of Laura, Nathan, Caralyn, Kara, and supporting cast members provides a sense of inspiration, comfort, and hope in the face of tragedy.

What did we witness and learn over the final twenty-seven months of Laura's life and afterward? How have the people involved adapted to life after Laura? The answers to these questions fulfill the purpose of this story.

Life for Laura and Nathan was good heading into 2011. They were planning their wedding and looking forward to a long and prosperous life together. In the blink of an eye, those plans changed on March 12, 2011. They aren't alone in life-changing events. It is the uniqueness of actions and sacrifices made by those affected in this story that gives us confidence there is a place for resiliency and compassion in this world.

Laura's survivorship was twice as long as the average time for her type of brain cancer. She underwent three major brain surgeries in fifteen months, two rounds of radiation therapy, and multiple administrations of different chemotherapy agents. She maintained a positive attitude throughout her treatment. Never once did she express sorrow for herself. Her courage was exceptional, only to be matched by her determination to live. She felt blessed to have Nathan as her husband and did all that she could to give him a child, all-the-while knowing she may never experience the feeling of motherhood. Laura taught us how to live in the face of extraordinary adversity.

Kara, with steadfast support from Aaron, gave Nathan,

the Brammeiers, Donna, and I the greatest gift: a beautiful granddaughter. She summarized her relationship with Laura in this way,

"It's hard to explain what having a best friend like Laura for twenty-four years meant to me. We were different enough and alike enough to get along perfectly. We were like sisters, soul mates, and best friends rolled into one." Kara showed us the meaning of unconditional friendship. She and her family remain close to both families and to Nathan and Caralyn. She will forever be Caralyn's birth mother. Kara continues to honor Laura's life when opportunities arise for her to do so. For Kara and her family, life goes on.

The medical care Laura received from Drs. Parney, Sandre and especially Dr. Uhm was best in class. Dr. Uhm and Nathan continue to communicate on a first-name basis. We are grateful for the care and support they gave to Laura. Dr. Uhm's medical knowledge, experience, and compassion serve as an example for all involved in healthcare. These physicians and their support teams deal with life-and-death situations on a daily basis. They save lives and continue the quest to find cures for dreaded illnesses. They taught us to seek out the best when confronted with the worst. For them, life goes on.

For the individuals, businesses, and organizations that provided support to Laura, Nathan, and Caralyn, you will never know how much your assistance meant to them and to us. You showed us the good in the world with your gifts, messages, and prayers. I have no doubt you will continue to support others in need, as life goes on.

There is no better group of people during difficult times than family. Turn to them for someone to talk to. They aid in carrying the burden. They do the little things that frequently go unnoticed and share in the emotions of the triumphs and setbacks. Since the birth of Caralyn, family members have made it a point—whether it be during a visit, a birthday, or over a holiday—to make her feel special. When the visits, birthdays, and holidays are over, they return to their own busy lives, and life goes on.

It's hard to imagine the conflicting emotions of Laura's parents and siblings in dealing with the loss of Laura and birth of Caralyn. Laura was a major part of their lives. She was the middle child and provided a sense of steadiness to her family. The grieving process never ends—it can't and shouldn't. It does become more regulated as time passes with certain activities or dates that trigger an emotional reaction. Laura can now be part of a conversation and draw a smile rather than tears. As Caralyn has gotten older, she helps fill the void and understands how loved her mother was by Grandma, Gramps, Joe, and Katy. As life goes on, she is now the focus of that love.

LIFE AFTER DEATH: THE LAURA AND CARALYN YOHO STORY

After Laura's passing and with the upcoming birth of Caralyn, Donna and I knew the trajectory of our lives would change. There were so many questions that would only be answered with the passage of time. Our task was to manage our grieving of Laura, prepare for the arrival of Caralyn, and offer support to Nathan in whatever way and for whatever situation he was dealing with.

Donna and I were raised by parents who put family first and sacrificed much. It was not a difficult decision to change our lifestyle. Caralyn would need a mother figure and Nathan a person to help with the daily duties as he began his business and to have someone available to have a conversation. Considering the circumstances, I felt we all did well adjusting to our new normal.

During the latter part of our stay with Nathan and Caralyn, I had several opportunities to leave Des Moines University for positions that would be considered promotions. One institution offered me a position that would fulfill my professional aspiration. Donna was excited about the opportunity. It was located close to family. When I approached Nathan about the position, he encouraged me to accept the offer. He also informed me it would be impossible for him to come along due to where he was with his business. I declined the offer. When I told Nathan about our decision, which was unanimous, he apologized. My response was easy. It wasn't because he would not come with us, it was because we weren't willing to leave them. And for us, life goes on.

Nathan was a pillar of strength for Laura and many others, from the time she was diagnosed to her death. Catching the falling candle stand at Laura's funeral was symbolic of his always being there. In a number of videos Nathan did for several local media outlets you could feel his sadness. It was on his face and in his words when he talked about Laura. At the same time, his demeanor about Caralyn was that of gratitude and happiness.

The first couple years after Laura's death, Nathan invested his time in raising Caralyn, building his business, and continuing to honor Laura through various charities. He eventually hit a wall. He talked less about Laura and focused on Caralyn and other business opportunities. It was during this time he sought help in the form of counseling with the grieving process. Regardless of how strong a person appears, having the ability to recognize you are struggling and need help is a sign of strength. After he completed counseling, conversations about Laura became more frequent. Caralyn had also reached an age where Nathan could keep another promise. He began to talk to her about Laura, showed her videos, and let her know how hard she tried to be with her. With Donna's help, he kept another promise:

to see that Caralyn had a relationship with Laura's family. It required much time and effort for Nathan to find peace and contentment so life could go on.

The circumstances that brought Caralyn into this world are both tragic and inspirational. Once the decision was made to use the IVF process and Kara as the surrogate, Caralyn as we know her, was destined by the grace of God to be with us in this world. She knows about her mother and that she died before she was born. She knows Kara is her birth mother. Caralyn is too young for us to even attempt to explain the science behind her birth. That will not happen until she asks.

Caralyn knows her circumstances are different than those of her cousins and friends. She is active, articulate, and athletic. She functions well in a group or one-on-one setting. She is also comfortable being by herself and letting her imagination guide her activities. As Caralyn grows and develops, she will continue to learn about herself, about this story, her story, as life goes on.

I have wondered what our lives would be like if Laura never had or was able to survive brain cancer. It's natural to have those fleeting "what if" moments, but that wasn't the outcome.

We are left to deal with reality and be thankful for the

blessing granted to us. Laura's headstone reads, "You made a difference."

Make the most of the life we are given and count for something, as Laura did in her short time on this earth.

For God so loved the world, that he gave his only begotten Son, that whosoever believeth in him should not perish, but have everlasting life (John 3:16)

Acknowledgements

I want to express my sincere appreciation to BobbiJo Wolfe, Robin Black, Ben Shirk of Shirk Photography, and Des Moines University for granting permission to use the photographs included in *Life After Death: The Laura and Caralyn Yoho Story*.

CPSIA information can be obtained
at www.ICGtesting.com
Printed in the USA
BVHW071029191221
624455BV00006B/213